Mediterranean Diet Cookbook

MEDITERRANEAN
-MAGIC-

The Complete Plant-Based Meal Plan Packed with Hearty Vegetables, Fruits, and Lean Meat For Weight Loss and Wellness

KEVIN OROZCO

from the Publisher. All additional right reserved.

The information in the following pages is broadly considered to be a truthful and accurate account of facts and as such any inattention, use or misuse of the information in question by the reader will render any resulting actions solely under their purview. There are no scenarios in which the publisher or the original author of this work can be in any fashion deemed liable for any hardship or damages that may befall them after undertaking information described herein.

Additionally, the information in the following pages is intended only for informational purposes and should thus be thought of as universal. As befitting its nature, it is presented without assurance regarding its prolonged validity or interim quality. Trademarks that are mentioned are done without written consent and can in no way be considered an endorsement from the trademark holder.

Table of Contents

PART I

Chapter 1: Identifying the Mediterranean Diet

We know that certain diets are associated with better health—this is a simple fact of life. We've seen that entire groups of people live longer based on where they live, and to some degree, a good deal of that has to come from somewhere—it has to come from something like diet or environment. In this case, the diet of the people living in the Mediterranean has been found to be incredibly healthy for people—it has been shown that people who are able to enjoy this diet, who are able to eat fresh food by the sea and enjoy the benefits that it has, are able to be far healthier than those who don't have it. That is great for them—but what is their secret?

It turns out, it's all in the lifestyle. The Mediterranean lifestyle, food, and all, is incredibly healthy for you. Studies have shown that people living in Mediterranean countries such as Greece and Italy have been found to have far less risk of death from coronary disease. Their secret is in the diet. Their diet has been shown to reduce the risk of cardiovascular disease, meaning that it is incredibly healthy, beneficial, and something that the vast majority of people in the world could definitely benefit from.

The Mediterranean diet is recommended by doctors and the World Health Organization as being not only healthy but also sustainable, meaning that it is something that is highly recommended, even by the experts. If you've found that you've struggled with weight loss, heart disease, managing your blood pressure, or anything similar to those problems, then the Mediterranean diet is for you.

When you follow this diet, you are able to bring health back to your life and enjoy the foods while doing so. It's perfect if you want to be able to enjoy your diet without having to worry about the impacts that it will have on you.

Defining the Mediterranean Lifestyle

The Mediterranean diet is quite simple. It involves eating traditional foods based on one's location. Typically, in the Mediterranean, that is a diet that is rich in veggies, fruits, whole grains, beans, and features olive oil as the fat of choice. Typically, it involves elements beyond just eating as well. While it is important to have healthy food, it is equally important to recognize that the diet encompasses the lifestyle as well. In particular, you can expect to see a few other rules come into play.

In particular, the Mediterranean diet is unique in the sense that it encourages a glass of red wine every now and then. In fact, the diet is associated with moderate drinking, enjoying red wine several times per week, always responsibly, and in contexts that will be beneficial to the drinker. If you want to be able to enjoy the Mediterranean diet and you are pregnant, or against drinking, you can do that, too—but traditionally, the red wine is included and even encouraged in moderation thanks to the antioxidants within it.

Additionally, on the Mediterranean diet, it is common to share meals with friends and family. This is essential—eating is more than just filling the body, it is nurturing the mind and relationships as well. This also comes with the added benefit of also being able to slow down eating—when you are eating the foods on this diet, you will discover that ultimately, you eat less when you're busy having a riveting conversation with someone. The fact that you are slowed down with your eating means that you will fill up sooner and realize that you didn't have to actually eat the food that you did. This means that you eat less and are, therefore managing your portions better as a result.

Finally, the Mediterranean diet focuses on physical activity. Traditionally, you would have had to go out to get the foods that you would eat each day, and that would mean that you'd need to get up, fish, garden, farm, or otherwise prepare your food. Eating locally is still a major component of this diet, as is getting up and being active. You need at least 30 minutes of activity, moderate or mild, per day. Even just walking for half an hour is better than nothing!

The Rules of the Mediterranean Diet

To eat the Mediterranean way, there are a few key factors that can guide you. If you know what you are doing, you can eat well without having to sacrifice flavor for health, and that matters immensely. When you look at the Mediterranean diet closely, you see that there are several tips that will help you to recognize what you need to do to stick to your diet.

Eating fruits and veggies

First, make sure that the bulk of your calories come from fruits and vegetables. You should be eating between 7 and 10 servings of fresh fruits and vegetables every single day—meaning that the bulk of your calories will come from there. Try to stick to locally grown foods that are fresh and in-season—they will have the highest nutritional value.

Reach for the whole grains

Yes, pasta is a major part of the diet in the Mediterranean, and you don't have to give that up entirely—but make sure that any grains that you are enjoying are whole-wheat. This allows you to enjoy foods that are high in fiber and are able to be digested differently than when you use refined carbs instead. While the refined carbs may give you instantaneous energy, they are also not nearly as good for you as whole wheat.

Using healthy fats

When it comes to flavoring or cooking your foods, you need to reach for the healthy fats first. This means choosing out foods that are cooked with olive oil instead of butter or dipping food in olive oil instead of butter. Olive oil, despite being a fat, has not been found to lead to weight gain when used in moderation. It is an incredibly healthy substitute for butter that is loaded up with all sorts of beneficial, heart-healthy antioxidants that will help your cardiovascular system.

Aim for seafood

When it comes to protein, fish, especially fresh fish, is the best choice. Fish should be consumed at least twice per week, and it should be fresh rather than frozen whenever possible. In particular, it is commonly recommended that you reach for salmon or trout, or other fatty fish because the omega-3 fatty acids within them are incredibly healthy for you, and they will serve you well. Even better, if you grill your fish, you have little cleanup.

Reduce red meat

In addition to adding more seafood to your diet, you need to cut out the red meat. The red meats in your diet are no good for you—they have been linked to inflammation that can make it harder for your cardiovascular system.

Enjoy dairy in moderation

When you are on this diet, dairy is not out of the picture entirely. While you should avoid butter, for the most part, it is a good idea for you to enjoy some low-fat Greek yogurt on occasion and add in some cheese to your diet. It is a good thing for you to enjoy these foods to ensure that you have plenty of calcium to keep your body strong.

Spices, not salt

Perhaps one of the most profound differences between most other diets and the Mediterranean diet is the lack of salt. The Mediterranean diet reaches for herbs and spices before adding in salt, meaning that you will be consuming less of it over time. Even better, you will grow to love your new foods without needing salt.

Chapter 2: Savory Mediterranean Meals

Mediterranean Feta Mac and Cheese

Ingredients

- Egg (1, beaten)
- Feta cheese (8 oz., crumbles)
- Macaroni (0.5 lb., whole-wheat)
- Olive oil (3 Tbsp.)
- Salt and pepper to taste
- Sour cream (8 oz.)

Instructions

1. Cook pasta to instructions to create al dente pasta. Drain and place pasta into baking dish. Toss in feta and oil and mix well.
2. Combine your egg and sour cream with salt and pepper. Then mix well and toss over macaroni. Combine and bake at 350F for 30 minutes.

Chickpea Stew

Ingredients

- Bay leaf (1)
- Dry chickpeas (1 c., soaked overnight and peeled)
- Garlic (1 clove, cut in half)
- Lemon to serve

- Olive oil (0.25 c.)
- Onion (1, diced)
- Salt and pepper to taste

Instructions

1. Cover chickpeas in pot with just enough water to cover them and wait to boil. Then rinse and set into clean pot. Toss in all other ingredients but the lemon with just enough water to cover nearly one inch above the beans. Simmer for 2-3 hours and serve with lemons.

Savory Mediterranean Breakfast Muffins

Ingredients

Dry ingredients

- Baking powder (1.5 tsp)
- Baking soda (o.5 tsp)
- Flour (2 c.)
- Salt (0.5 tsp)

Wet ingredients

- Egg (1 large)
- Garlic (1 clove, minced)
- Milk (1 c.)
- Sour cream (0.25 c.)
- Vegetable oil (0.25 c.)

Fillings

- Cheddar cheese (2 c., shredded)
- Feta (2.5 oz., crumbled)
- Green olives (diced, 0.5 c.)
- Green onions (0.5 c., chopped)
- Roasted red peppers (0.5 c., chopped)
- Sun dried tomatoes (diced, 0.5 c.)

Instructions

1. Combine dry ingredients in a bowl. Mix wet ingredients in separate bowl. Combine the two together and mix.
2. Toss in fillings in as few stirs as possible.
3. Place in greased or lined muffin pan, dividing to all 12 recesses.
4. Bake for 25 minutes until golden-brown and crusty at 350F.
5. Cool for 10 minutes and serve warm.

Mediterranean Breakfast Bake

Ingredients

- Artichoke hearts (14-oz. can, drained)
- Bread (6 slices whole-wheat, chopped)
- Eggs (8)
- Feta cheese (0.5 c.)
- Italian sausage (turkey or chicken—1 lb., casings removed)
- Milk (1 c.)
- Olive oil (2 Tbsp., divided)

- Onion (1, chopped)
- Spinach (5 oz.)
- Sun dried tomato (1 c., chopped)

Instructions

1. Warm 1 Tbsp. of your olive oil on moderately high heat. Cook sausage for 8 minutes until it has browned, breaking it up as it cooks. Place it in a dish when it is done.
2. Toss in additional oil, then cook onion until soft, roughly 5 minutes. Toss in spinach until wilting (1 minute).
3. Combine eggs and mix in milk, bread, tomatoes, cheese, artichokes, sausage, and finally, the spinach mix.
4. Place everything in a 2.5 quart baking dish. Let sit for an hour in fridge, or leave overnight.
5. Let casserole sit for 30 minutes after removing from fridge. Then, bake for 45 minutes at 350F until brown. Let rest 10 minutes, then serve.

Mediterranean Pastry Pinwheels

Ingredients

- Cream cheese (8-ounce package, softened)

- Pesto (0.25 c.)

- Provolone cheese (0.75 c.)

- Sun-dried tomatoes (0.5 c., chopped)

- Ripe olives (0.5 c., chopped)

Instructions

1. Unroll pastry and trim it up to create 10-inch square.

2. Mix together your cream cheese and pesto until well-combined. Then, mix in other ingredients until combined. Place mixture in even layer across pastry, up to 0.5-inch of edges. Roll and freeze for 30 minutes.

3. Cut whole roll into 16 pieces.

4. Bake at 400F until golden, roughly 15 minutes. Serve.

Chapter 3: Sweet Treats on the Mediterranean Diet

Greek Yogurt Parfait

Ingredients

- Almond butter (2 Tbsp.)
- Fresh fruit (1 Tbsp.)
- Greek Yogurt (1 c.)

Instructions

1. Mix together yogurt and 1 Tbsp. of almond butter and put in a bowl. Top with fruit.
2. Warm remaining butter in microwave for 10 minutes, then drizzle atop yogurt. Serve. You can add different toppings to change up the flavor as well.

Overnight Oats

Ingredients

- Chia seeds (1 Tbsp.)

- Greek yogurt (0.25 c.)

- Honey (1 Tbsp.)

- Milk of choice (0.5 c.)

- Old fashioned whole oats (0.5 c.)

- Vanilla extract (0.25 tsp)

Instructions

1. Mix all ingredients into a glass container and leave in fridge for at least 2 hours but preferably overnight. Serve with berries of choice or other desired toppings.

Apple Whipped Yogurt

Ingredients

- Greek yogurt (1 c.)
- Heavy cream (0.5 c.)
- Honey (1 Tbsp.)
- Unsalted butter (2 Tbsp.)
- Apples (2, cored and chopped into small bits)
- Sugar (2 Tbsp.)
- Cinnamon (1/8 tsp)
- Walnut halves (0.25 c., chopped)

Instructions

1. Using a hand mixer, mix together yogurt, honey, and honey until it creates peaks.
2. Heat up your butter in a skillet over a moderate temperature. Cook apples and 1 Tbsp. sugar in pan. Stir and cook for 6-8 minutes until soft. Then, top with the rest of sugar and cinnamon, stirring and cooking an additional 3 minutes. Take it off of the burner and let it rest for 5 minutes.
3. Serve with whipped yogurt in bowl topped with apple, then sprinkle on walnuts.

Chapter 4: Gourmet Meals on the Mediterranean Diet

Garlic-Roasted Salmon and Brussels Sprouts

Ingredients

- Brussels sprouts (6 c., trimmed and halved)
- Chardonnay (0.75 c.)
- Garlic cloves (14 large)
- Olive oil (0.25 c.)
- Oregano (2 Tbsp., fresh)
- Pepper (0.75 tsp)
- Salmon fillet (2 lbs., skin-off—cut in 6 pieces)
- Salt (1 tsp)
- Lemon wedges to serve

Instructions

1. Take two cloves of garlic and mince, combining them with oil, 1 Tbsp. of oregano, half of the salt and 1/3 of the pepper. Cut remaining cloves of garlic in halves and toss them with the sprouts. Take 3 Tbsp. of your garlic oil and toss it with the sprouts in roasting pan. Roast for 15 minutes at 450F.

2. Add wine to the remainder of the oil mixture. Then, remove it from the pan, stir veggies, and place salmon atop it all. Pour the wine mix atop it and season with remaining oregano and salt and pepper. Bake 5-10 minutes until salmon is done. Serve alongside the wedged lemon.

Walnut Crusted Salmon with Rosemary

Ingredients

- Dijon mustard (2 tsp)
- Garlic (1 clove, minced)
- Honey (0.5 tsp)
- Kosher salt (0.5 tsp)
- Lemon juice (1 tsp)
- Lemon zest (0.25 tsp.)
- Olive oil (1 tsp)
- Olive oil spray
- Panko (3 Tbsp.)
- Red pepper (0.25 tsp)
- Rosemary (1 tsp, chopped)

- Salmon (1 pound, skin removed)
- Walnuts (3 Tbsp., finely chopped)
- Parsley and lemon to garnish

Instructions

1. Mix together the mustard, lemon zest and juice, honey, salt and red pepper, and rosemary. In a separate dish, combine the panko with oil and walnuts.
2. Spread mustard across salmon and top with panko mixture. Spray fillets with cooking spray.
3. Cook until fish begins to flake at 425F, roughly 8-10 minutes. Serve with lemon and parsley.

Spaghetti and Clams

Ingredients

- Clams (6.5 lbs.)
- Olive oil (6 Tbsp.)
- White wine (0.5 c.)
- Garlic (3 cloves, sliced)
- Chiles (3, small and crumbled)
- Spaghetti (1 lb.)
- Parsley (3 Tbsp., chopped)
- Salt and pepper to personal preference

Instructions

1. Prepare clams, soaking in clean water and brushing to remove all sand.

2. Warm 2 Tbsp. of oil in large pot. Then, toss in 0.25 c. wine, 1 of the cloves of garlic, and 1 chile. Cook half of the plans at high heat with regular shaking until clams are opened. Remove opened clams and their juices to a larger bowl. Repeat process with second half of clams. Discard any that do not open.

3. Prepare pasta according to packaging to create al dente pasta. Reserve 1 c. pasta water.

4. Warm remainder of oil (2 Tbsp.) in pot over moderate heat, tossing in remainder of garlic and chile. Cook until fragrant, then place all clams and their juices into the pot, tossing to coat well. Then, toss in pasta, mixing well to combine. If necessary, add in cooking liquid. Serve and season with salt/pepper to personal preference with parsley atop.

Braised Lamb and Fennel

Ingredients

- Bay leaves (2)
- Chicken broth (3 c.)
- Cinnamon stick (1)
- Fennel (1 bulb, chopped)
- Garlic head (chopped in half)
- Lamb shoulder (3 lbs., cut into 8 pieces)
- Olive oil (2 Tbsp.)
- Onion (1, chopped
- Orange (1 with peel, cut into wedges)
- White wine (1 c.)
- Whole peeled tomatoes (14.5 oz. can)

Instructions

1. Dry lamb and season with salt and pepper to taste. Warm oil inside a Dutch oven, and sear lamb on all sides, roughly 6 minutes each side. Move lamb to plate.
2. Place fennel, garlic, and onion in the pot and cook, until browning, roughly 8 minutes. Mix in wine and boil, deglazing the pan. Reduce heat and simmer until it has reduced 50%.
3. Toss in orange, bay leaves, tomatoes, broth, and cinnamon, plus the lamb. Simmer, then cover pot and transfer to oven set to 325F. braise for 1.5-2 hours. Remove lamb and place on clean plate.
4. Strain liquid left in pot, then return it to the pot to boil until thick, roughly 30 minutes.
5. Return lamb to pot to warm. Serve.

Mediterranean Cod

Ingredients

- Black olives (0.66 c., sliced)
- Cod (4 fillets, skinless)
- Fennel seeds (1 tsp)
- Lemon (1, sliced)
- Lemon (juice of ½ lemon)
- Olive oil (6 Tbsp.)
- Onion (1, sliced)
- Parsley (1 Tbsp., chopped)
- Salt and pepper to personal preference
- Tomatoes (0.66 c., diced)

Instructions

1. Warm olive oil at a moderate temperature, sautéing the onion with a pinch of salt until translucent, roughly 10 minutes.
2. Mix in tomato and olives, tossing in the juice as well. Allow it to simmer gently for roughly 5 minutes. Toss in fennel seeds and set aside.
3. Warm the rest of the oil in another pan and fry up the cod for 10 minutes, flipping halfway through until done.
4. Toss tomato sauce over heat to warm, then mix together the parsley, and serve atop the cod with a lemon slice.

Baked Feta with Olive Tapenade

Ingredients

- Baked pita or crusty bread to serve
- Feta cheese (6 oz.)
- Garlic (2 cloves)
- Green olives (0.33 c., sliced)
- Harissa paste (3 Tbsp.)
- Olive oil (3 Tbsp.)
- Parsley (3 Tbsp., fresh chopped)
- Roasted red peppers (16-oz. jar, drained)
- Salt (0.75 tsp.)
- Tomato paste (2 Tbsp.)
- Walnuts (0.5 c., halved)

Instructions

1. In a blender, combine your peppers, 0.25 c. walnuts, harissa and tomato paste, garlic, and 0.5 tsp of your salt until mostly consistent. It doesn't have to be perfect, but should be well combined.

2. Take half of mixture into baking dish that has been sprayed with cooking spray. Top with half of your feta, then spoon the rest of the red pepper sauce atop it.

3. Top with the last of the feta and bake until bubbly, roughly 25 minutes. Broil for the last 2.

4. While that bakes, make your tapenade. This requires you to combine your remaining ingredients together.

5. Remove mixture from oven and top with tapenade. Serve immediately with crusty bread or pita chips.

Chapter 5: 30-Minutes or Less Meals

Vegetarian Toss Together Mediterranean Pasta Salad

Ingredients

- Artichoke hearts (12 oz. jar, drained)
- Balsamic vinegar (2 Tbsp.)
- Kalamata olives (12-ounce jar, drained and chopped)
- Olive oil (2 Tbsp.)
- Pasta (8 oz., wheat)
- Salt to personal preference
- Sun-dried tomatoes in oil (1.5 oz. jar, drained)

Instructions

1. Prepare pasta according to packaging.

2. Mix together olives, tomatoes, and artichoke.

3. Drain pasta and add them to a bowl with artichoke mixture. Then, top with vinegar and olive oil, mix well, and serve warm.

Vegetarian Aglio e Olio and Broccoli

Ingredients

- Olive oil (3 Tbsp.)
- Cayenne peppers (3)
- Garlic (3 cloves, sliced)
- Broccoli (1 head, prepared in florets)
- Spaghetti (7 oz. whole wheat)
- Salt to taste

Instructions

1. Boil water and prepare spaghetti according to instructions until al dente. Drain and reserve.

2. In a pan, heat up 1 Tbsp. of your olive oil at a moderate temperature, then toss in the garlic and peppers, sautéing until fragrant. Remove garlic from heat and set aside.

3. Toss broccoli into pan and cook for 4 minutes. Then toss in spaghetti, garlic, and remaining oil. Cook for an additional minute or two, then serve.

Cilantro and Garlic Baked Salmon

Ingredients

- Cilantro (stems trimmed)
- Garlic (4 cloves, chopped)
- Lime (0.5, cut into rounds)
- Lime juice (1 lime's worth)
- Olive oil (0.5 c.)
- Salmon fillet (2 pounds, skin removed)
- Salt to taste
- Tomato (cut into rounds)

Instructions

1. Allow salmon to come to room temp for 20 minutes while oven preheats to a temperature of 425 F.
2. While you wait, take a processor and combine garlic, cilantro, lime juice, and olive oil with a pinch of salt. Combine well.
3. Place fillet into baking pan that has been greased. Top with a light sprinkle of salt and pepper. Then spread cilantro sauce atop fillet, coating whole salmon. Top with tomato and lime.
4. Bake for 6 minutes per 0.5 inch of thickness (1-inch fillets take around 8-10 minutes). Let rest for 5-10 minutes out of the oven. Serve.

Harissa Pasta

Ingredients

- Pasta (2 cups)
- Red bell pepper (1)
- Red onion (1)
- Pine nuts (2 Tbsp.)
- Harissa paste (2 Tbsp.)

Instructions

1. Roast onions and peppers with olive oil at 400F for 20 minutes. Remove from oven and dice.
2. Prepare pasta to instructions on package. While pasta cooks, toast your pine nuts until browned in frying pan.
3. Drain pasta, leaving a touch of the water. Then, add in diced roasted veggies and harissa. Serve topped with pine nuts.

Chapter 6: 1-Hour-or-Less Meals

1 Hour Baked Cod

Ingredients

- Basil (0.5 tsp., dried)
- Bay leaf (1)
- Capers (1 small jar)
- Cod fillets (2 pounds)
- Fennel seeds (1 tsp., crushed)
- Garlic (1 clove, minced)
- Lemon juice (0.25 c., fresh)
- Olive oil (2 tsp)
- Onion (1, sliced)
- Orange juice (o.25 c., fresh)
- Orange peel (1 Tbsp.)
- Oregano (0.5 tsp., dried)
- Salt and pepper to personal preference
- White wine (1 c., dry)
- Whole tomatoes (16-oz. can, chopped and reserving juice)

Instructions

1. Warm oven to 375F.
2. In cast iron skillet, warm oil. Then, sauté your onion for 5 minutes. At this point, mix in all other ingredients but fish. Allow to simmer for 30 minutes.
3. Place fillets into skillet and top with most of the sauce. Allow to bake for 15 minutes until fish flakes.

Grilled Chicken Mediterranean Salad

Ingredients

- Artichoke hearts (0.33 c., chopped)
- Balsamic vinegar (2 Tbsp.)
- Basil (1 tsp, dried)
- Chicken breasts (3, cut into bite-sized chunks)
- Cucumber (0.75 c., diced)
- Feta cheese (0.25 c.)
- Garlic (1 clove, minced)
- Greek yogurt (2 Tbsp.)
- Green onions (0.25 c., chopped)

- Kalamata olives (3 Tbsp., sliced)
- Kosher salt (0.5 tsp)
- Lemon juice (3 Tbsp + 1 tsp.)
- Olive oil (3 Tbsp. + 2 Tbsp.)
- Onion powder (0.5 tsp)
- Parsley (0.5 tsp)
- Pesto (4 tsp)
- Pinch of red pepper
- Roasted red pepper (6 Tbsp., sliced)
- Romaine (4 c., chopped)
- Shiitake mushrooms
- Spinach (4 c., chopped)
- Tomato (0.75 c., diced)
- White wine vinegar (4 tsp)

Instructions

1. Create your salad. Each plate should have a bed of romaine and spinach, topped with cucumber, tomato, artichoke, peppers, olives, and cheese.
2. Combine your tsp of lemon juice, wine vinegar, and pesto in a jar and shake to combine. Then, add in yogurt and 2 Tbsp. oil, mixing well until well-incorporated.
3. Prepare your chicken. Let it marinade in a mixture of 3 Tbsp. lemon juice, balsamic vinegar, remaining oil, and all seasonings for at least 30 minutes. Soak some wooden skewers in water during this time.
4. Make kebabs out of chicken and mushroom, alternating bite of chicken and bite of mushroom until chicken is gone. Grill for 10 to 15 minutes until done.
5. Drizzle salad with the vinaigrette, then place a kebab atop each. Serve.

Lemon Herb Chicken and Potatoes One Pot Meal

Ingredients

- Baby potatoes (8, halved)
- Basil (3 tsp, dried)
- Bell pepper (1, seeds removed and wedged)
- Chicken thighs (4, skin and bone on)
- Garlic (4 large cloves, crushed)
- Kalamata olives (4 Tbsp., pitted)
- Lemon juice (1 lemon's worth)
- Olive oil (3 Tbsp.)
- Oregano (2 tsp, dried)

- Parsley (2 tsp, dried)

- Red onion (wedged)

- Red wine vinegar (1 Tbsp.)

- Salt (2 tsp)

- Zucchini (1 large, sliced)

- Lemons for garnish

Instructions

1. Combine juice from lemon, 2 Tbsp. olive oil, vinegar, seasonings, and garlic into dish. Pour half to reserve for later, then place chicken in half. Let sit for 15 minutes (or overnight if you would like to prep the day before)

2. Warm oven to 430F. Sear chicken in cast iron skillet in remaining olive oil, about 4 minutes per side. Drain all but 1 Tbsp. of fat.

3. Place all veggies around the thighs. Top with remaining marinade and combine well to cover everything.

4. Cover pan and bake for 35 minutes until soft and chicken is to temperature. Then, broil for 5 minutes or until golden brown. Top with olives and lemon to serve.

Vegetarian Mediterranean Quiche

Ingredients

- Butter (2 Tbsp.)
- Cheddar cheese (1 c., shredded)
- Eggs (4 large)
- Feta (0.33 c.)
- Garlic (2 cloves, minced)
- Kalamata olives (0.25 c., sliced)
- Milk (1.25 c.)
- Onion (1, diced)
- Oregano (1 tsp, dried)
- Parsley (1 tsp, dried)
- Pie crust (1, prepared)
- Red pepper (1, diced)
- Salt and pepper to personal preference
- Spinach (2 c., fresh)
- Sun dried tomatoes (0.5 c.)

Instructions

1. Soak sun-dried tomatoes in boiling water for 5 minutes before draining and chopping.
2. Prepare a pie dish with a crust, fluting the edges.
3. In a skillet, melt your butter, then cook your garlic and onions in it until they become fragrant. Combine in the red peppers for another 3 minutes until softened. Then, toss in your spinach, olives, and seasoning. Cook until the spinach wilts, about 5 minutes. Take it off of the heat and toss

in your feta and tomatoes. Then, carefully place mixture into the crust, spreading it into a nice, even layer.

4. Mix milk, eggs, and half of cheddar cheese together. Pour it into the crust. Then, top with cheddar.

5. Bake for 50 minutes at 375 f. until crust is browned and egg is done.

Herbed Lamb and Veggies

Ingredients

- Bell pepper (2, any color, seeds removed and cut into bite-sized chunks)
- Lamb cutlets (8 lean)
- Mint (2 Tbsp., fresh, chopped)
- Olive oil (1 Tbsp.)
- Red onion (1, wedged)
- Sweet potato (1 large, peeled, and chunked)
- Thyme (1 Tbsp., fresh, chopped)
- Zucchini (2, chunked)

Instructions

1. Assemble your veggies onto a baking sheet and coat with oil and black pepper. Bake at 400F for 25 minutes.
2. As veggies bake, trim fat from the lamb. Then, combine the herbs with a bit of freshly ground pepper. Coat the lamb in the seasoning.
3. Remove veggies, flip, and push to one side of pan. Then, arrange your cutlets onto the baking pan as well. Bake for 10 minutes, flip, then cook an additional 10 minutes. Combine well, then serve.

Chicken and Couscous Mediterranean Wraps

Ingredients

- Parsley (1 c., fresh and chopped)
- Olive oil (3 Tbsp.)

- Garlic (2 tsp, minced)
- Salt (pinch)
- Pepper (pinch)
- Chicken tenders (1 pound)
- Tomato (1, chopped)
- Cucumber (1, chopped)
- Spinach wraps (4 1o-inch)
- Water (0.5 c)
- Mint (0.5 c., fresh chopped)
- Lemon juice (0.25 c.)
- Couscous (0.33 c.)

Instructions

1. Cook couscous in boiling water according to directions on package.
2. Mix together your lemon juice, oil, garlic, salt and pepper, mint, and parsley.
3. Coat chicken in 1 Tbsp. of your mixture from previous step and top with a pinch of salt. Cook in skillet until completely cooked, usually just a few minutes per side.
4. Wait for chicken to cool, then chop into bites.
5. Pour the remainder of your parsley mixture into the couscous with cucumbers and tomato bits.
6. Place 0.75 c. of couscous mixture into a tortilla, then spread chicken atop it, rolling them up and serving.

Sheet Pan Shrimp

Ingredients

For shrimp

- Feta cheese (0.5 c.)
- Fingerling potatoes (2 c., halved)
- Green beans (6 oz., trimmed)
- Olive oil (3 Tbsp.)

- Pepper (1 tsp)
- Red onion (1 medium, sliced)
- Red pepper (1 medium, sliced)
- Salt (1 tsp)
- Shrimp (1 lb., deveined and peeled)

For Marinade

- Garlic (1 Tbsp., minced)
  Oregano (0.5 tsp)
- Greek yogurt (1 c.)
- Lemon juice (2 Tbsp.)
- Paprika (0.5 tsp)
- Parsley (2 Tbsp., chopped)

Instructions

1. Combine all marinade ingredients and set aside.
2. Take shrimp in a bowl with 0.5 c. of the marinade. Let them sit for 30 minutes.
3. During rest time, set up your baking sheet with foil or parchment, and prepare your veggies. Chop them up and toss onto baking sheet, drizzling them with the olive oil and giving them a quick sprinkle of salt and pepper. Bake for roughly 20 minutes at 400F, then remove from oven. Take out all green beans and set to the side.
4. Place shrimp in one layer across the pan and bake for an additional 10 minutes until shrimp is done. Serve with veggies and shrimp in bowls, topped with 2 Tbsp. feta and a spoonful of yogurt marinade.

Mediterranean Mahi Mahi

Ingredients

- Basil (6 leaves, freshly chopped)
- Capers (4 Tbsp.)
- Garlic (2 cloves, chopped)
- Italian seasoning (pinch)
- Kalamata olives (25, chopped)
- Lemon juice (1 tsp)
- Mahi mahi (1 pound)
- Olive oil (2 Tbsp.)
- Onion (o.5, chopped)
- Parmesan cheese (3 Tbsp.)
- Diced tomatoes (15 oz. can)
- White wine (0.25 c.)

Instructions

1. Warm olive oil in a pan and then cook onions until translucent. Toss in garlic and seasoning and stir to mix well. Then, add in your can of tomatoes, wine, olives, lemon, and roughly half of the chopped basil. Drop heat down and toss in parmesan cheese. Cook until bubbling.
2. Put fish into a baking pan, then top with the sauce. Bake for 20 minutes at 425 F until fish is to temperature.

Chapter 7: Slow Cooker Meals

Slow Cooker Mediterranean Chicken

Ingredients

- Bay leaf (1)
- Capers (1 Tbsp.)
- Chicken broth (0.5 c.)

- Chicken thighs (2 pounds, bone and skin removed)
- Garlic (3 cloves, minced)
- Kalamata olives (1 c.)
- Olive oil (1 Tbsp.)
- Oregano (1 tsp)
- Roasted red pepper (1 c.)
- Rosemary (1 tsp, dried)
- Salt and pepper to taste
- Sweet onion (1, thinly sliced)
- Thyme (1 tsp, dried)
- Optional fresh lemon wedges to juice for serving

Instructions

1. Sauté the chicken in olive oil to brown on both sides, then remove it from the pan. Then, sauté the onions and garlic as well until beginning to soften, roughly 5 minutes.
2. Put chicken, onion, garlic, and all other ingredients into a slow cooker and leave it to cook for 4 hours on low. Season to taste.

Slow Cooker Vegetarian Mediterranean Stew

Ingredients

- Carrot (0.75 c., chopped)
- Chickpeas (15 oz. can)
- Crushed red pepper (0.5 tsp)
- Fire-roasted diced tomatoes (2 14-oz. cans)
- Garlic (4 cloves, minced)
- Ground pepper (0.25 tsp)
- Kale (8 c., chopped)

- Lemon juice (1 Tbsp.)
- Olive oil (3 Tbsp.)
- Onion (1, chopped)
- Oregano (1 tsp)
- Salt (0.75 tsp)
- Vegetable broth (3 c.)
- Basil leaves (garnish)
- Lemon wedges (garnish)

Instructions

1. Mix tomatoes, onion, carrot, broth, seasonings, and garlic into the slow cooker. Cook on low for 6 hours.
2. Take out 0.25 c. of the liquid in the slow cooker after 6 hours and transfer it to a bowl. Take out 2 Tbsp. of chickpeas and mash them with the liquid until nice and smooth.
3. Combine mash, kale, juice from lemon, and whole chickpeas. Cook for about 30 minutes, until kale is tender, then serve garnished with the basil leaves and lemon wedges.

Vegetarian Slow Cooker Quinoa

Ingredients

- Arugula (4 c.)
- Chickpeas (1 15.5 oz. can, rinsed and drained)
- Feta cheese (0.5 c)
- Garlic (2 cloves, minced)
- Kalamata olives (12, halved)
- Kosher salt (0.75 tsp)
- Lemon juice (2 tsp)
- Olive oil (2.25 Tbsp.)
- Oregano (2 Tbsp., fresh and coarsely chopped

- Quinoa (1.5 c., uncooked)
- Red onion (1 c., sliced)
- Roasted red pepper (0.5 c., drained and chopped)
- Vegetable stock (2.25 c.)

Instructions

1. Mix your broth with the onion, garlic, quinoa, chickpeas, and 1.5 tsp of olive oil. Sprinkle half of the salt atop it. Mix and cook on low until quinoa is done, roughly 3 or 4 hours.
2. Turn off the slow cooker and mix well. In a separate bowl, combine remaining olive oil, salt, and lemon juice together. Then, mix that into the slow cooker, along with the peppers.
3. Combine in the arugula and leave until the greens start to wilt. Serve, topping with feta, oregano, and olives.

Slow-Cooked Chicken and Chickpea Soup

Ingredients

- Artichoke hearts (14 oz. can, drained and chopped)
- Bay leaf (1)
- Cayenne (0.25 tsp)
- Chicken thighs (2 lbs., skins removed)
- Cumin (4 tsp)
- Diced tomatoes (1 15-ounce can)
- Dried chickpeas (1.5 c., allow to soak overnight)
- Garlic cloves (4, chopped)
- Olives (o.25 c., halved)
- Paprika (4 tsp)
- Pepper (0.25 tsp)
- Salt (0.5 tsp)

- Tomato paste (2 Tbsp.)
- Water (4 c.)
- Yellow onion (chopped)
- Parsley or cilantro (garnish)

Instructions

1. Drain your soaked chickpeas and place them into your slow cooker (large preferred). Mix in the water, onions and garlic, tomatoes (undrained), tomato paste, and all seasonings. Combine well, then add in the chicken.

2. Leave it to cook for 8 hours at low, or 4 at high.

3. Remove the chicken and allow it to cool on a cutting board. At the same time, remove the bay leaf, then add in the artichoke and olives. Season with additional salt if necessary to taste. Chop up chicken, removing the bones, and then mix it back into the soup. Serve the soup with the parsley or cilantro garnishing the top.

Slow Cooked Brisket

Ingredients

- Beef broth (0.5 c.)
- Brisket (3 lbs.)
- Cold water (0.25 c.)
- Fennel bulbs (2, cored, trimmed, and cut into wedges)
- Flour
- Italian seasoning (3 tsp)
- Italian seasoning diced tomatoes (14.5 oz. can)
- Lemon peel (1 tsp., fine shreds)
- Olives (0.5 c.)
- Parsley for garnish
- Pepper (pinch)
- Salt (pinch)

Instructions

1. Trim meat, then season with 1 tsp Italian seasoning. Put it in slow cooker with the cut-up fennel on top.
2. Mix together the tomatoes, broth, peel, olives, salt and pepper, and the last of the Italian seasoning.
3. Cook at low for 10 hours, or high for 5.
4. Take meat out of the cooker and reserve all juice. Arrange meat with veggies on a serving platter.
5. Remove fat from top of the juices.
6. Take 2 c. of juices in saucepan. Mix together water and flour, then combine it into the juice. Cook until gravy forms.
7. Serve meat topped with gravy and garnish with parsley.

Vegan Bean Soup with Spinach

Ingredients

- Vegetable broth (3 14-oz. cans)
- Tomato puree (15 oz. can)
- Great Northern or White beans (15 oz. can)
- White rice (0.5 c)
- Onion (0.5 c., chopped)
- Garlic (2 cloves, minced)
- Basil (1 tsp., dried)
- Pinch of salt
- Pinch of pepper
- Kale or spinach (8 c., chopped)

Instructions

1. Mix everything but leafy greens together in your slow cooker. Cook for 5 or 7 hours on low, or 2.5 hours on high.
2. Toss in leafy greens. Wait for them to wilt and serve.

Moroccan Lentil Soup

Ingredients

- Carrots (2 c., chopped)
- Cauliflower (3 c.)
- Cinnamon (0.25 tsp)
- Cumin (1 tsp)
- Diced tomato (28 oz.)
- Fresh cilantro (0.5 c.)
- Fresh spinach (4 c.)
- Garlic (4 cloves, minced)
- Ground coriander (1 tsp)
- Lemon juice (2 Tbsp.)
- Lentils (1.75 c.)

- Olive oil (2 tsp)
- Onion (2 c., chopped)
- Pepper (pinch)
- Tomato paste (2 Tbsp.)
- Turmeric (1 tsp)
- Vegetable broth (6 c.)
- Water (2 c.)

Instructions

1. Mix everything but spinach, cilantro, and lemon juice. Cook until lentils soften. This will be 4-5 hours if you use high heat, or 10 hours on low.
2. Mix spinach when just 30 minutes remains on cook time.
3. Just before serving, top with cilantro and lemon juice.

Chapter 8: Vegetarian and Vegan Meals

Vegetarian Greek Stuffed Mushrooms

Ingredients

- Cherry tomatoes (0.5 c., quartered)
- Feta cheese (0.33 c.)
- Garlic (1 clove, mixed)
- Ground pepper (0.5 tsp)
- Kalamata olives (2 Tbsp.)
- Olive oil (3 Tbsp.)
- Oregano (1 Tbsp., fresh and roughly chopped)
- Portobello mushrooms (4, cleaned with stems and gills taken out)
- Salt (0.25 tsp)
- Spinach (1 c., chopped)

Instructions

1. Begin by setting your oven. This recipe requires 400F for baking.
2. Mix together your salt and 0.25 tsp pepper, garlic, and 2 Tbsp. of oil, and use it to cover your mushrooms, inside and out.
3. Set the mushrooms onto your baking pan and allow it to cook for 10 minutes.
4. Mix together your remaining ingredients and combine well. Then, when the mushrooms are done, remove them from the oven and then fill them up with your filling.
5. Allow to cook for another 10 minutes.

Vegetarian Cheesy Artichoke and Spinach Stuffed Squash

Ingredients

- Artichoke Hearts (10 oz., frozen—thawed and chopped up)

- Baby spinach (5 oz.)

- Cream cheese (4 oz., softened)

- Parmesan cheese (0.5 c.)

- Pepper (pinch to taste)

- Red pepper and basil (for garnish)

- Salt (pinch to taste)
- Spaghetti squash (1, cut in half and cleaned out of seeds)
- Water (3 Tbsp.)

Instructions

1. Microwave your squash, flat side down, with 2 Tbsp. of your water uncovered for 10-15 minutes.
2. Mix together your spinach and water into a skillet until they begin to wilt. Then drain and reserve for later.
3. Preheat your oven set to broil with the rack at the upper 1/3 point.
4. Remove flesh from squash with a fork, then place the shells onto a sheet for the oven. Then stir in your artichoke, cheeses, and a pinch of salt and pepper to the squash flesh. Combine thoroughly, then split it between the two shells. Broil for 3 minutes and top with red pepper and basil to taste.

Vegan Mediterranean Buddha Bowl

Ingredients

For the chickpeas

- Chickpeas (1 can, rinsed, drained, and skinned)
- Olive oil (1 tsp)
- Pinch of salt and pepper
- Dried basil (0.25 tsp)
- Garlic powder (0.25 tsp)

For the quinoa

- Quinoa (0.5 c.)
- Water (1 c.)

For the salad

- Bell pepper (1, color of choice, seeded, stemmed, and chopped to bite-sized bits)
- Cucumbers (2, peeled and chopped)
- Grape tomatoes (1 c., halved)
- Hummus (0.5 c.)
- Kalamata olives (0.5 c.)
- Lettuce (2 c. – can sub in field greens, spinach, kale, or any other leafy greens)

Instructions

1. Set your oven up to prepare for baking. It should be at 0400F. Then, mix the ingredients for the chickpeas together, coating them evenly with the seasoning.
2. Put chickpeas in single layer and put them onto the baking sheet. Roast for 30 minutes with an occasional mixing and rotation of the pan to allow them all to cook evenly. Allow them to cool.
3. Start preparing the quinoa and water in a microwave-safe bowl. Combine the water and quinoa and microwave, covered, for 4 minutes. Then stir and microwave for 2 minutes longer. Give it one final stir and leave it to rest in the microwave for another minute or two.
4. Begin assembling your salad. Begin with the greens at the bottom, then top with tomatoes, cucumbers, bell pepper, olives, chickpeas, and then quinoa. Finally, top with a dollop of hummus to serve.

Vegan Mediterranean Pasta

Ingredients

- Artichokes (0.5 c.)
- Basil leaves (0.25 c., torn)
- Garlic cloves (2-3 to taste, minced)
- Grape tomatoes (2 c., halved)
- Kalamata olives (10, pitted)
- Olive oil (1 Tbsp.)

- Pasta (8 oz.)
- Red pepper (o.25 tsp.)
- Salt and pepper to taste
- Spinach (4 c.)
- Tomato paste (4 Tbsp.)
- Vegetable broth (1 c.)

Instructions

1. Prepare your pasta based on the instructions provided. Keep 1 c. of the water for later use and then set the pasta aside.

2. While preparing your pasta, take the time to warm a large skillet with oil. Then, sauté your garlic and red pepper for 30 seconds or so. Combine in the tomato paste and cook for another minute. At that point, mix in your tomatoes, your seasoning, your artichokes and olives, and your broth. Let it cook until tomatoes start to break down.

3. Mix in the pasta to the tomato mixture. Let it cook another 2 minutes and add reserved pasta water if too dry.

4. Add in spinach and basil and cook until wilted.

5. Remove from heat and serve.

Vegetarian Zucchini Lasagna Rolls

Ingredients

- Basil (2 Tbsp., fresh)
- Egg (1, lightly beaten)
- Frozen spinach (10-ounce package, thawed and dried)
- Garlic (1 clove)
- Marinara sauce (0.75 c.)
- Olive oil (2 tsp)
- Parmesan cheese (3 Tbsp.)
- Pinch each of salt and pepper
- Ricotta (1.33 c.)
- Shredded mozzarella cheese (8 Tbsp.)
- Zucchini (2, trimmed)

Instructions

1. Prepare two baking sheets with cooking spray. Then set the oven to 425F.
2. Cut up your zucchini into strips lengthwise into 1/8 inch thick pieces. A mandolin will make this easier.
3. Prepare zucchini coated in oil with salt and pepper, then set up a flat layer across the bottom of the prepared pan.
4. Bake zucchini for 10 minutes until it begins to soften.
5. Mix together 2 Tbsp. mozzarella and 1 Tbsp. of parmesan. Then, in another bowl, combine egg, ricotta, spinach, garlic, and the remainder of the cheese. Toss in a pinch of salt and pepper and mix well.
6. Set up an 8-inch square casserole dish with 0.25 c. marinara spread across the bottom.
7. Take your zucchini that has been softened and begin to roll it. To do this, you will need to put 1 Tbsp. of ricotta mix at the bottom of your strip, then roll. Put the seam down in the marinara-covered bottom. Do this for all pieces of zucchini.
8. Cover the rolls with the remainder of your marinara sauce and top with the cheese mix.
9. Bake until bubbling, roughly 20 minutes. Rest for 5 minutes and top with basil.

Vegetarian Breakfast Sandwich

Ingredients

- Sandwich thins (2)
- Olive oil (2 Tbsp. + 1 tsp)
- Rosemary (1 Tbsp. fresh, or 0.5 tsp dried)

- Eggs (2)
- Spinach leaves (1 c.)
- Tomato (0.5, sliced thinly)
- Feta (2 Tbsp.)
- Pinch of salt and pepper

Instructions

1. Warm oven to 375F. Separate your sandwich thins and coat with olive oil. Bake for 5 minutes until beginning to crisp up.
2. Warm skillet with last tsp of olive oil. Break eggs into pan and cook until whites are set. Then, break the yolks and flip to finish cooking.
3. Put bottoms of the bread onto serving plates. Then, top with spinach, the tomato, one egg each, followed by the feta. Sprinkle with salt and pepper, then top with remaining bread.

Vegan Breakfast Toast

Ingredients

- Bread of choice (verify that it is vegan—2 slices)
- Spice blend of choice
- Arugula (handful)
- Tomato (1, cut into rounds)
- Chopped olives (1 Tbsp.)
- Cucumber (0.5, cut into rounds)
- Hummus (0.25 c.)

Instructions

1. Toast up your bread. Then spread the hummus across, season it, and top with all toppings split between the pieces.

Vegetarian Shakshouka

Ingredients

- Chopped parsley (1 Tbsp.)
- Diced Tomatoes (15 oz. can)
- Eggs (4)
- Garlic (2 cloves)

- Olive oil (2 Tbsp.)

- Onion (1—sliced)

- Red bell peppers (2, sliced thinly)

- Salt and pepper to taste

- Spicy harissa (1 tsp)

- Sugar (1 tsp)

Instructions

1. Warm oil in a cast iron pan. Sauté your peppers and onions until they have begun to soften, giving them a stir every now and then to prevent sticking. Add in the garlic for another minute.

2. Put in tomatoes, sugar, and harissa, leaving it to simmer for the next 7 minutes.

3. Season it to taste. Then, add in small indentations into the mixture in the pan, cracking an egg in each indentation that you make. Cover up the pot and allow it to cook until egg whites are done.

4. Cover with parsley and serve with bread.

PART II

Chapter 1: Introduction to the Heart-Healthy Diet

A heart-healthy diet is incredibly important. The truth is, you must be able to manage your diet well if you want to be healthy. The average diet is actually incredibly unhealthy for the heart, and the sooner that you are able to change up how you treat yourself and your body, the better off you will be. The average person consumes far too much salt and not enough of the important fruits and veggies that they need. As a result, they wind up with problems with their blood sugars, their blood pressure, and cholesterol levels. It is important to understand that your heart is one of the most important parts of your body—you cannot live without it. You need to keep it healthy. If you want to ensure that you can keep yourself healthy, you need to make sure that you eat the foods that will help you to nourish it readily. The sooner that you can do so, the better off you will be. This book is here to provide you with plenty of heart-healthy meals that you can enjoy that will help you to stay as healthy as possible.

The Rules of the Heart-Healthy Diet

Before we begin, let's go over some of the most important rules that go into the heart-healthy diet. These are rules that will help you to ensure that your body is kept as healthy as possible with foods that will nourish you well. Now, on this diet, you can expect to follow these rules:

1. **Decrease saturated and trans fats:** These are fats that are no good for anyone. Instead, it is recommended that you focus entirely on monounsaturated and polyunsaturated fats. These come from primarily

vegetarian options—common sources include olive and canola oils, avocado, nuts, and fatty fish.

2. **Increase fruits and veggies:** Your body needs the vitamins and minerals in fruits and veggies to stay as healthy as possible. You should be consuming at least seven to nine servings per day to keep your body healthy and on track.

3. **Consume more fiber:** Typically, on this diet, you want to up your fiber intake. Fiber is necessary to keep your body regular. It also helps with the way that you will naturally digest and absorb nutrients. You need both soluble and insoluble sources to stay as healthy as possible. Soluble fiber will aid in regulating your body and is fantastic for the heart. Insoluble fiber is there to help you regulate your weight and pass waste.

4. **Make the switch to plant proteins whenever possible:** You will also see that this diet advocates for more vegetarian options and less meat. While you can still eat meat, it is highly recommended that you choose to put in at least three servings of vegetable proteins, and you limit red meats down to just once a week. Twice a week, you should eat skinless poultry, and twice a week, you should enjoy fish.

5. **Up your whole grain intake:** This is essential to ensuring that you are not just consuming a bunch of empty carbs that aren't doing anything for you. By shifting to whole grains, you get more of the fiber that you need, and they are also usually full of better nutritional content as well.

6. **Limiting sweets:** If you are going to enjoy sweets, it is usually recommended that you cut out sugar or sugar-sweetened dishes. While

you do not have to completely eliminate them, you should, at the very least, monitor and regulate intake.

7. **Low-fat dairy products:** You should have between two and three servings of dairy per day, but they ought to be reduced fat.

8. **Drink in moderation:** Alcohol is okay—but is not really encouraged either. If you must drink alcohol, make sure that you do so in moderation, which is typically defined as no more than one per day for women and no more than two per day for men.

The Benefits of the Heart-Healthy Diet

The heart-healthy diet has all sorts of benefits that are worth enjoying, and you should be able to treat these as motivation. If you find that you are struggling to enjoy this diet, consider these benefits to give you that added boost. Ultimately, the heart is the key to the body, and if you can keep it healthier, you will enjoy a better life for reasons such as:

*   **Preventing heart disease:** When you limit salts, sweets, red meats, and everything else, you will help your heart remain healthier, and in doing so, you will reduce your risk of both stroke and heart disease.

*   **Keeping your body healthier:** This diet is often recommended to older people, and this is for good reason—it keeps the body more agile by reducing the risk of frailty and muscle weakness.

- **Cutting the risk of Alzheimer's disease:** This diet helps your cholesterol, blood sugar, and blood vessel health, all of which are believed to aid in reducing the risk of both dementia and Alzheimer's disease.

- **Cutting the risk of Parkinson's disease:** Similarly, because this diet will be high in antioxidants, it has been found to cut the risk of Parkinson's disease significantly.

- **Longer lifespan:** This diet, because it lowers your risk of heart disease and cancer, is actually able to reduce your risk of death by around 20%.

- **Healthier mind:** If you suffer from anxiety or depression, this diet can actually help to alleviate some of the symptoms, or keep them at bay in the future. Between the healthy fats, rich vegetable content, and the boost to your gut bacteria, you will find that your body and mind both are healthier than ever.

- **It helps manage weight:** If you have struggled with your weight for some time, you may find that using this diet will actually help you to manage it, thanks to the fact that you'll be cutting out much of the foods that tend to lead to weight gain in the first place. You'll be able to enjoy a healthier body as the weight fades away through enjoying this diet.

Chapter 2: Heart-Healthy Savory Meals

Shrimp Scampi and Zoodles

Ingredients

- Butter (1 Tbsp., unsalted)
- Dry white wine (0.5 c.)
- Garlic (4 cloves, grated)
- Lemon juice (2 Tbsp.)
- Lemon zest (1 Tbsp.)
- Linguini (6 oz.)
- Olive oil (2 Tbsp.)
- Parsley (0.25 c., chopped)
- Red pepper flakes (0.25 tsp.)
- Shrimp (1.5 lbs., peeled and deveined—preferably large)
- Zucchini (3, spiralized)

Instructions

1. Start by preparing the pasta based on the instructions on the package. Keep 0.25 c. of the water to the side and drain the rest. Put pasta back in the pot.
2. Combine the shrimp, garlic, oil, salt, and pepper to taste and allow it to sit for five minutes.
3. Prepare a skillet and cook your shrimp in the garlicky oil over medium and garlic until done, roughly 3-4 minutes per side with a large count. Move shrimp to plate without the oil.
4. Add zest and pepper to the oil, along with the wine. Scrape the brown bits and reduce to 50%. Mix in lemon juice and butter, then toss the zoodles in.
5. After 2 minutes, add in shrimp, pasta, and combine well. Mix in water if necessary and toss with parsley.

Citrus Chicken Salad

Ingredients

- Baby kale (5 oz.)

- Chicken thighs (2 lbs.)

- Dijon mustard (1 tsp)

- Lemon juice (2 Tbsp.)

- Olive oil (2 Tbsp.)

- Orange (1, cut into 6 pieces)

- Salt and pepper

- Stale bread (8 oz., torn up into bite-sized bits)

Instructions

1. Warm oven to 425F. As it preheats, warm up half of your oil into a skillet. Then, salt and pepper the chicken, cooking it skin-side down in the oil. After 6 or 7 minutes, when the skin is golden, remove it to a baking sheet. Then, toss in the orange wedges and roast another 10 minutes until the chicken is completely cooked.

2. Reserve 2 Tbsp. of the chicken fat in the pot and then return it to low heat. Toss in the bread chunks, coating them in the fat. Add a quick sprinkle of salt and pepper, then cook until toasted, usually about 8 minutes or so. Set aside.

3. Warm pan on medium-low, then toss in lemon juice. Deglaze the pan for a minute, then remove from heat. Combine with Dijon mustard and juice from roasted oranges. Mix in remaining oil.

4. Add kale and croutons to skillet to mix well, coating it in the mixture. Serve immediately with chicken.

Shrimp Taco Salad

Ingredients

- 3 Fresh lime juice (3 tbsp.)
- Avocado (1)
- Cayenne pepper sauce (1 tsp.)
- Cilantro leaves (1 c.)
- Corn chips (such as Fritos-- 2 c.)
- Extra-virgin olive oil (0.25 c.)
- Fresh corn (3 pieces)
- Ground coriander (0.25 tsp.)
- Ground cumin (0.25 tsp.)
- Salt
- Shrimp (1 lb.)
- Watermelon (2 c.)
- Zucchini (2 medium)

Instructions

1. Set up your grill to medium heat.
2. First grill the corn until it begins to char, usually about 10 minutes, with the occasional turn. At the same time, allow zucchini to grill for around 6 minutes until beginning to soften. Shrimp requires 2-4 minutes until cooked through, flipping once.
3. Combine your oil, juice, and seasonings, with just a pinch of salt.
4. Remove the kernels off of your corn and slice up your zucchini. Place zucchini and avocado onto a plate, topping it with the corn, then the watermelon, and finally the shrimp. You can leave it as is until you're ready to eat—it keeps for about a day in the fridge.
5. To serve, top with the chips (crumbled) and the dressing mix.

Chicken, Green Bean, Bacon Pasta

Ingredients

- Bacon (4 slices)

- Chicken breast (1 lb., cut into bite-sized bits)

- Egg yolk (1 large)

- Green beans (fresh—8 oz., trimmed and cut in half)

- Half-and-half (2 Tbsp.)

- Lemon juice (2 Tbsp.)

- Parmesan cheese (1 oz., grated—about 0.5 c.)

- Penne pasta (12 oz.)

- Scallions (2, sliced thinly)

- Spinach (5 oz.)

Instructions

1. Prepare pasta according to the package. Then, at the last minute of cooking, toss in the beans. Drain, reserving 0.5 c. of the cooking water. Leave pasta mix in the pot.

2. In a skillet, start preparing the bacon until crisp. Dry on a paper towel and then break into bits when cooled. Clean pan, reserving 1 Tbsp. of bacon fat.

3. On medium heat, cook the chicken until browning and cooked all the way. Then, off of the burner, toss in the lemon juice.

4. Mix together your egg and half-and-half in a separate container. Then, dump it to coat in the pasta and green beans, then toss in the chicken, spinach, and cheese. Mix well to coat. Add pasta water if needed, 0.25 c. at a time. Mix in the scallions, then top with bacon. Serve.

Heart-Healthy "Fried" Chicken

Ingredients

- Blackening seasoning (2 tsp.)
- Buttermilk (0.5 c.)
- Chicken drumsticks (2 lb., skinless)
- Cornflakes (4 c.)
- Olive oil (1 Tbsp.)
- Parsley (0.5 c., chopped)
- Salt (a pinch to taste)

Instructions

1. Get ready to bake the chicken at a temperature of 375F and make sure that you've got something to bake on that is currently protected.
2. Mix buttermilk, seasoning, and a touch of salt.
3. Crush cornflakes and put them in a second bowl. Combine with the oil and parsley.
4. Prep chicken by dipping first in buttermilk, letting it drip, then coating in cornflakes. Bake for 30-35 minutes.

Turkey Burgers and Slaw

Ingredients

Slaw

- Apple (1, matchstick-cut)
- Cabbage (8 oz., thinly sliced)
- Honey (1 Tbsp.)
- Jalapeno (1, thinly sliced and seeded)
- Lime juice (3 Tbsp.)
- Red wine vinegar (1 Tbsp.)
- Salt and pepper, to your preference

Burgers

- Buns (4, toasted lightly)
- Chili paste (1.5 Tbsp.)
- Ginger (1 Tbsp., grated)
- Olive oil (2 Tbsp.)
- Onion (0.5 chopped)
- Soy sauce (1 Tbsp.)
- Turkey (1 lb., ground up)

Instructions

1. Mix together the liquids for the slaw and the seasoning. Mix well, then toss in the slaw ingredients. Set aside.
2. Prepare your burger mixture, adding everything together, but the oil and the buns somewhere that you can mix them up. Combine well, then form four patties.
3. Prepare to your preference. Grills work well, or you choose to, you could use a cast iron pan with the oil. Cook until done.
4. Serve on buns with slaw and any other condiments you may want.

Slow Cooked Shrimp and Pasta

Ingredients

- Acini di pepe (4 oz., cooked to package specifications)
- Basil (0.25 c., chopped fresh)
- Diced tomatoes (14.5 oz. can)
- Feta (2 oz., crumbled)
- Garlic (2 cloves, minced)
- Kalamata olives (8, chopped)
- Olive oil (1 Tbsp.)
- Pinch of salt
- Rosemary (1.5 tsp fresh, chopped)
- Shrimp (8 oz., fresh or frozen)
- Sweet red bell pepper (1, chopped)
- White wine (0.5 c.) or chicken broth (o.5 c.)
- Zucchini (1 c., sliced)

Instructions

1. Thaw, peel, and devein shrimp. Set aside in fridge until ready to use them.

2. Coat your slow cooker insert with cooking spray, then add in tomato, zucchini tomatoes, bell pepper, and garlic.

3. Cook on low for 4 hours, or high for 2 hours. Mix in shrimp. Then, keep heat on high. Cook covered for 30 minutes.

4. Prepare pasta according to the instructions on the packaging.

5. Mix in the olives, rosemary, basil, oil, and salt.

6. Serve with pasta topped with shrimp, then topped with feta.

Chapter 3: Heart-Healthy Sweet Treats

Chocolate Mousse

Ingredients

- Avocado (1 large, pitted and skinned)
- Cocoa powder (2 Tbsp., unsweetened)
- Nondairy milk of choice (3 Tbsp., unsweetened)
- Nonfat vanilla Greek yogurt (0.25 c.)
- Semi-sweet baking chocolate (2 oz., melted and cooling)
- Sweetener packet if desired.
- Vanilla extract (1 tsp.)

Instructions

1. Prepare by putting all ingredients but sugar into a food processor. Combine well. Taste. If you want it sweeter, add in some sweetener as well.
2. Chill in your fridge until you are ready to serve.

Baked Pears
Ingredients

- Almonds (0.25 c., chopped)
- Brown sugar (0.33 c., can sub with honey)
- Butter (2 oz., melted, or coconut oil if you prefer vegan)
- Ground cinnamon (1 tsp)
- Ripe pears (3)
- Rolled oats (0.5 c.)
- Salt (a pinch)
- Sugar (pinch)

Instructions

1. Set oven to 400 F.
2. Incorporate all dry ingredients. Then, mix half of your melted butter.
3. Cut your pears in half and carve out the cores, making a nice scoop in the center. Brush with butter, then top with a sprinkle of sugar.
4. Put your cinnamon oat mixture into the centers of the pears.
5. Bake for 30-40 minutes, until soft.

Chocolate Peanut Butter Bites
Ingredients

- Chocolate chips of choice (2 c.)
- Coconut flour (1 c.)
- Honey (0.75 c.)
- Smooth peanut butter (2 c.)

Instructions

1. Prepare a tray with parchment paper to avoid sticking or messes
2. Melt together your peanut butter and honey, mixing well
3. Add coconut flour to peanut butter mixture and combine to incorporate. If it's still thin, add small amounts of flour. Let it thicken for 10 minutes.
4. Create 20 balls out of the dough.
5. Melt chocolate, then dip the dough balls into the chocolate and place them on the parchment. Refrigerate until firm.

Oatmeal Cookies

Ingredients

- Applesauce (2.5 Tbsp.)
- Baking soda (0.25 tsp)
- Coconut oil (2 Tbsp., melted)
- Dark chocolate chips (0.25 c.)
- Honey (0.25 c.)
- Salt (0.5 tsp)
- Vanilla extract (2 tsp.)
- Whole grain oats (0.5 c.)
- Whole wheat flour (0.5 c.)

Instructions

1. Set your oven to 350 F.
2. Mix syrup, oil (melted), applesauce, and vanilla.
3. Toss in salt, baking soda, oats, and flour. Combine well until it becomes a dough.
4. Mix the chocolate chips in.
5. Put in tablespoons onto cookie sheet.
6. Bake for 10 minutes. Let cool before transferring to a cooling rack.

Pina Colada Frozen Dessert

Ingredients

- Butter (0.25 c.)
- Crushed pineapple in juice (undrained—1 8 oz. can)
- Graham cracker crumbs (1.25 c.)
- Rum extract or rum (0.25 c.)
- Sugar (1 Tbsp.)
- Toasted flaked coconut (0.25 c.)
- Vanilla low-fat, no-sugar ice cream (4 c.)

Instructions

1. Prepare oven to 350 F.
2. Combine butter, cracker crumbs, and sugar. Press into a 2-quart baking dish. Bake 10 minutes and allow to cool completely
3. Combine ice cream, pineapple and juice, and extracts into a bowl with a mixer until well combined. Spread it out into the crust.
4. Freeze for 6 hours.
5. Serve after letting thaw for 5 minutes and topping with coconut shreds.

Kiwi Sorbet

Ingredients

- Kiwi (1 lb., peeled and frozen)
- Honey (0.25 c.)

Instructions

1. Combine everything well in a food processor until mixed.
2. Pour it into a loaf pan and smooth it out.
3. Allow it to freeze for 2 hours. Keep it covered if leaving it overnight in the freezer.

Ricotta Brûlée

Ingredients

- Ricotta cheese (2 c.)
- Lemon zest (1 tsp)
- Honey (2 Tbsp.)
- Sugar (2 Tbsp.)

Instructions

1. Mix together your ricotta, lemon zest, and honey. Then, split into ramekins. Top with sugar and place onto baking sheet.
2. Place oven rack at the topmost position then set the baking sheet in with the broiler on its highest setting. Watch closely and broil until it bubbles and turns golden brown—between 5 and 10 minutes.
3. Cool for 10 minutes and top with any fruits or toppings you prefer.

Chapter 4: Heart-Healthy Gourmet Meals

Grilled Halibut With Pine Nut Relish
Ingredients

- Diced red tomato (0.5 c.)
- Diced yellow tomato (o.5 c)
- EVOO (3 Tbsp.)
- Flour to coat fish
- Green olives (0.5 c.)
- Halibut fillet (4, 1 inch thick)
- Kalamata olives (0.5 c.)
- Lemon juice (1 Tbsp.)
- Zest from a lemon (0.5 tsp.)
- Parsley (2 Tbsp.)
- Pepper to taste
- Pine nuts (3 Tbsp.)
- Salt (pinch to taste)
- Shallot (1)

Instructions

1. Start with toasting the pine nuts in a dry skillet for a few minutes until toasted. Set aside.
2. Combine your tomatoes, the sliced olives, shallot, the lemon juice and zest, and 1 Tbsp. of oil. Mix well and add in parsley and a sprinkle of pepper.
3. Flour fillets, shaking off excess. Season lightly with salt and pepper. Toss the rest of your oil into your skillet and use that to cook the fish until done, flipping halfway over.
4. Serve with relish on top and garnish with pine nuts.

Shrimp Bowls

Ingredients

- Avocado (1, cut small)
- Broccoli (1 lb., florets)
- Ginger (1 Tbsp.)
- Olive oil (2 Tbsp.)
- Plum tomatoes (8 oz., seeds removed and cut)
- Quinoa (1.5 c.)
- Rice vinegar (1 Tbsp.)
- Salt and pepper to taste
- Scallions (2, thinly sliced)
- Shrimp (20 large, peeled and deveined)

Instructions

1. Warm oven to 425 F. Prepare medium saucepan at medium heat and cook the quinoa until toasted, roughly 5 minutes. Add in water (3 c.), then cover immediately. Allow it to cook just below a boil for 10 minutes, then take it off the burner and let it sit for another ten minutes.
2. On a baking sheet, add broccoli, 1 Tbsp. oil, salt, and pepper. Prepare in a single layer. Roast for 15 minutes. Season shrimp, then cook for 6-8 minutes, tossed with broccoli.
3. Mix vinegar, ginger, and remaining oil into a small bowl. Toss with tomatoes and scallions.
4. Serve with quinoa in bowls, topped with broccoli shrimp, then avocado. Finally, add the vinaigrette to the top.

Grilled Watermelon Steak Salad

Ingredients

- Cherry tomatoes (1 lb., halved)
- Honey (1 tsp)
- Lemon juice (3 Tbsp.)
- Mint leaves (1 c., torn up)
- Olive oil (2 Tbsp.)
- Onion (0.5 tsp., small red)
- Parsley (1 c., chopped)
- Salt and pepper
- Sirloin steak (1 lb.)
- Unsalted peanuts to garnish
- Watermelon (3 lbs., seedless)

Instructions

1. Prepare grill to medium-high. Season steak, then grill until done to preference. Allow it to rest on a cutting board.
2. Mix oil, lemon juice, honey, and seasonings. Incorporate the onions and tomatoes as well, folding in nicely.
3. Cut watermelon into 0.5-inch thick triangles and remove rinds. Oil and grill until starting to char—a minute per side, then set aside.
4. Mix the herbs into the tomato mixture. Serve with watermelon topped with stead.

Crispy Cod and Green Beans

Ingredients

- Green Beans (1 lb.)
- Olive oil (2 Tbsp.)
- Parmesan cheese (0.25 c., grated)
- Pepper to taste
- Pesto (2 Tbsp.)
- Salt to taste
- Skinless cod (1.25 lb., four pieces)

Instructions

1. Set oven to 425 F. Put beans onto rimmed baking sheet and combine with 1 Tbsp. oil, then top with cheese and a sprinkling of seasonings. Roast for 10-12 minutes, waiting for it to finally start to brown.

2. Heat remaining oil in a skillet. Season cod and cook until golden brown. You want to use a medium-high heat to do this.

3. Serve with pesto over cod, next to a bed of green beans.

Pistachio-Crusted Fish

Ingredients

- Baby spinach (4 c.)
- Greek yogurt (4 Tbsp.)
- Lemon juice (2 Tbsp.)
- Olive oil (2 Tbsp.)
- Panko (whole-wheat, 0.25 c.)
- Pepper (0.5 tsp)
- Quinoa (0.75 c.)
- Salt (0.75 tsp)
- Shelled pistachios, chopped (0.25 c.)
- Tilapia (4 6-oz. pieces)

Instructions

1. Prepare quinoa based on instructions on packaging.
2. Season fish with salt, pepper, and coat with 1 Tbsp. each of Greek yogurt.
3. Combine panko and pistachios, tossing with 1 Tbsp. olive oil. Gently sprinkle over the top of the fish, pressing it to stick. Bake for 12 minutes at 375 F., or until done.
4. Combine cooked quinoa with spinach, lemon juice, remaining oil, and a pinch of salt and pepper. Serve with fish.

Cumin-Spiced Lamb and Salad

Ingredients

- Carrots (1 lb.)
- Cumin (1.25 tsp.)
- Honey (0.5 tsp.)
- Lamb loin chops (8—about 2 lbs.)
- Mint leaves (0.25 c., fresh)
- Olive oil (3 Tbsp.)
- Radishes (6)
- Red wine vinegar (2 Tbsp.)
- Salt and pepper to taste

Instructions

1. Combine 2 Tbsp. oil, vinegar, a pinch of cumin, honey, and salt and pepper.
2. Warm remaining oil in a skillet at medium. Season lamb with cumin and a pinch of salt and pepper. Cook until preferred doneness.
3. Shave carrots into pieces and create thinly sliced radishes. Coat with dressing and mix with mint. Serve with lamb.

Chapter 5: Heart-Healthy Quick 'n Easy Meals

Sugar Snap Pea and Radish Salad

Ingredients

- Apple-cider vinegar (2 Tbsp.)
- Avocado (0.5, medium ripe)

- Dijon mustard (0.5 tsp)
- Fresh lemon juice (1 Tbsp.)
- Freshly ground pepper (0.5 tsp)
- Ground coriander (0.25 tsp)
- Olive oil (0.25 c.)
- Radishes (12, small)
- Salt (o.5 tsp)
- Sugar snap peas (1 lb.)
- Watermelon radish (1, small)

Instructions

1. Combine peas and radishes in a bowl together.
2. In a blender, combine everything else and puree until well combined and smooth. Add water if necessary to thin it out.
3. Coat radish and peas with dressing and serve.

Horseradish Salmon Cakes

Ingredients

- Dijon mustard (1 Tbsp.)
- English cucumber (1, small)
- Greek Yogurt (2 Tbsp.)
- Horseradish (2 Tbsp.)
- Lemon juice (1 Tbsp.)
- Olive oil (2 Tbsp.)
- Panko (0.25 c.)
- Salt and pepper to taste
- Skinless salmon filet (1.25 lb.)
- Watercress (1 bunch)

Instructions

1. Combine salmon, horseradish, salt and pepper, and mustard into a food processor until well chopped. Then, toss in the bread crumbs and combine well.
2. Form 8 patties.
3. Warm 1 Tbsp. oil in a skillet. Cook until opaque throughout, typically 2 minutes before flipping.
4. Combine yogurt, lemon juice, oil, and a sprinkle of salt and pepper. Combine in cucumber slices, then watercress.
5. Serve salmon with salad.

Salmon, Green Beans, and Tomatoes

Ingredients

- Garlic (6 cloves)
- Green beans (1 lb.)
- Grape tomatoes (1 pint)
- Kalamata olives (0.5 c.)
- Anchovy fillets (3)
- Olive oil (2 Tbsp.)
- Kosher salt and pepper to personal preference
- Salmon fillet, skinless

Instructions

1. Prepare oven to 425 F. Put beans, garlic, olive, anchovy, and tomatoes together along with half of the oil and a pinch of pepper. Roast until veggies are tender.

2. Warm the remainder of the oil over a skillet at medium heat. Season salmon, then cook until done. Serve salmon and veggies together.

Broccoli Pesto Fusilli

Ingredients

- Basil leaves (0.5 c.)
- Broccoli florets (12 oz.)
- Fusilli (12 oz.)
- Garlic (2 cloves)
- Lemon zest (1 Tbsp.)
- Olive oil (3 Tbsp.)
- Parmesan cheese to garnish
- Salt to taste
- Sliced almonds to garnish

Instructions

1. Prepare pasta to directions and reserve 0.5 c. of the liquid.
2. Combine broccoli, garlic, and the reserved water in a bowl and cook for five or six minutes, stirring halfway through. Put everything right into a food processor with the liquid. Combine in basil, oil, zest, a pinch of salt, and puree.
3. Put pasta in with pesto. Drizzle in water if necessary. Sprinkle with cheese and nuts if desired. Serve immediately.

Strawberry Spinach Salad

Ingredients

- Baby spinach (3 c.)
- Medium avocado (0.25, diced)
- Red onion (1 Tbsp.)
- Sliced strawberries (0.5 c.)
- Vinaigrette of choice (2 Tbsp.)
- Walnut pieces (roasted)

Instructions

1. Combine spinach with the berries and onion. Mix well. Coat with vinaigrette and toss. Then, top with walnuts and avocado. Serve.

One-Pot Shrimp and Spinach

Ingredients

- Crushed red pepper (0.25 tsp)
- Garlic (6 cloves, sliced)
- Lemon juice (1 Tbsp.)
- Lemon zest (1.5 tsp.)
- Olive oil (3 Tbsp.)
- Parsley (1 Tbsp.)
- Salt to personal preference
- Shrimp (1 lb.)
- Spinach (1 lb.)

Instructions

1. Warm skillet with 1 Tbsp. oil. Cook half of the garlic until browning, about a single minute. Then, toss in spinach and salt. Wait for it to wilt over the heat, about 5 minutes. Remove and mix in lemon juice, storing it in a separate bowl.
2. Warm heat to medium-high and toss with remainder of oil. Toss in the rest of your garlic and cook until browning. Then, mix in shrimp, pepper, and salt. Cook until shrimp is done, then serve atop spinach with lemon zest and parsley garnish.

Chapter 6: Heart-Healthy Vegetarian and Vegan Meals

Vegetarian Butternut Squash Torte
Ingredients

- Butternut squash (1 lb.)
- Crusty bread of choice
- Kale (1, small)
- Olive oil (1 Tbsp.)
- Parmesan cheese (4 Tbsp., grated)
- Plum tomato (1)
- Provolone cheese (6 oz., thinly sliced)
- Red onion (1, medium)
- Salt and pepper to taste
- Yukon Gold potato (1, medium)

Instructions

1. Take a spring form 9-inch pan and prepare it so that nothing will stick. Then, take your squash and put it around the bottom in circles to sort of mimic a crust.
2. Then, layer it with the onion, with the rings separated out.
3. Add half of your kale, then sprinkle half of your oil, and season to taste.
4. Then, layer with potatoes, half of your cheese, and top with the last of your kale.
5. Add the oil, onion, tomato slices, and the last of your cheese.
6. Top it with the remainder of your squash, then coat with parmesan.
7. Bake, covering the top with foil, for 20 minutes. Then, discard the foil and let it bake until it is tender and browning, typically another ten minutes or so.

Vegetarian Fried Rice

Ingredients

- 2 eggs (leave out if vegan)
- Garlic (2 cloves, pressed)
- Kale (6 oz., thinly sliced leaves)
- Olive oil (1 Tbsp.)
- Rice (4 c., cooked and chilled, preferably the day before)
- Sesame oil (1 Tbsp.)
- Shiitake mushroom caps (4 oz., sliced)
- Soy sauce (2 Tbsp., low sodium)
- Sriracha (1 tsp.)

Instructions

1. Start by warming your oil up in your pan of choice or wok. Your oil should be just before the smoking point.
2. Cook the mushrooms and toss until they start to turn golden brown, usually just a few minutes, then set them off for later.
3. Toss in some sesame oil and kale, cooking until wilted, then add in your garlic as well for another minute.
4. Take your rice and mix it in as well, tossing it together until heated.
5. Move all rice to the side, then pour beaten eggs in the center of your pan. Stir often until the eggs are just about finished, and then mix into the rice.
6. Mix in the soy sauce and sriracha, then top with mushrooms.

Ingredients

- Butternut squash (1, 2.5 lbs. with skin and seeds removed—keep seeds)

- Carrots (2 medium, cut into 1-inch pieces)

- Coconut milk (2 Tbsp.)

- Olive oil (2 Tbsp., and one tsp)

- Onion (1, large, chopped)

- Pepper (2.25 tsp)

- Turmeric (2.25 tsp)

- Veggie bouillon base (1 Tbsp.)

Instructions

1. Take a Dutch oven and add 2 Tbsp. oil. Warm, then cook your onions until soft and translucent, roughly 6 minutes or so.

2. Integrate your bouillon base with 6 c., boiling water until completely dissolved.

3. Toss together your veggies, turmeric, and pepper into your onions in the Dutch oven. Allow it to cook for a minute before mixing in your veggie broth. Simmer for 20 minutes until veggies are soft.

4. Turn your oven to 375F. Take your seeds and your oil that is remaining and combine them together. Then, coat it up with the turmeric and pepper before toasting in your oven for about 1o minutes.

5. With a blender or immersion blender, combine your soup until smooth.

6. Serve topped with seeds and a swirl of coconut milk.

Vegetarian Kale and Sweet Potato Frittata

Ingredients

- Eggs (6)
- Garlic (2 cloves)
- Goat cheese (3 oz.)
- Half-and-half (1 c.)
- Kale (2 c., packed tightly)
- Olive oil (2 Tbsp.)
- Pepper (0.5 tsp.)
- Red onion (0.5, small)
- Salt (1 tsp.)
- Sweet potatoes (2 c.)

Instructions

1. With your oven warming, combine your eggs in a bowl. Then, add in the salt and half-and-half as well. Make sure your oven is at 350F.

2. In a nonstick skillet that you can put into your oven, cook your potatoes over 1 Tbsp. of oil. Wait for them to soften and start to turn golden. Then, remove from the pan.

3. Next, cook your kale, onion, and garlic together in the remainder of your oil until it is wilted and aromatic.

4. Put your potato back in with the kale, then pour your egg mix atop it all. Incorporate well and then allow it to cook on the stove for another 3 minutes.

5. Top it all with the goat cheese, then bake for 10 minutes until completely done.

Vegan Ginger Ramen

Ingredients

- Garlic (4 cloves, minced)
- Ginger (0.33 c., chopped coarsely)
- Grapeseed oil (0.5 c.)
- Low-sodium soy sauce (2 Tbsp.)
- Pepper (1 tsp., freshly ground)
- Ramen noodles (*real,* fresh noodles—not the $0.10 packaged stuff)
- Rice vinegar (1 Tbsp.)
- Salt to personal preference
- Scallions (1 bunch—about 2 c. sliced)
- Sesame oil (1 tsp)
- Sugar (0.5 tsp)

Instructions

1. Combine your ginger with the minced garlic and roughly 60% of your scallions.
2. Warm up the grapeseed oil until just before the smoking point. Then, take the oil and dump it over your scallion mix. It will sizzle and wilt, turning green. Leave it for 5 minutes, then add in the rest of the scallions.
3. Carefully combine in soy sauce, sesame oil, vinegar, sugar, and pepper, and leave it to incorporate for the next 15 minutes or so. Adjust flavor accordingly.
4. Prepare your noodles to the package instructions. Drain.
5. Introduce your noodles to your scallion sauce and coat well.
6. Serve topped with sesame seeds or any other toppings you may want.

Vegan Glazed Tofu

Ingredients

- Canola oil (0.5 c.)
- Firm tofu (12 oz.)
- Ginger (0.5" sliced thinly)
- Maple syrup (3 Tbsp.—you can use honey if you're not vegan.)
- Pepper flakes (0.5 tsp.)
- Rice vinegar (3 Tbsp.)
- Soy sauce (4 Tbsp.)
- Toppings of choice—recommended ones include rice, scallions, or sesame seeds

Instructions

1. Dry and drain your tofu out, squeezing it between paper towels so that you can remove as much of the liquid as you possibly can, then slice it into cubes.
2. Combine the wet ingredients together, and add in your pepper and ginger.
3. Warm your wok or skillet. When the oil is shimmery, gingerly place your tofu into it carefully and leave it for around 4 minutes so that it can brown. It should be dark brown when you flip. Repeat on both sides. Then, drop the heat down and toss in your sauce mix. Allow it to reduce until it is thick, roughly 4 minutes.
4. Put tofu on plates and top with anything you desire.

Vegan Greek Tofu Breakfast Scramble

Ingredients

- Basil (0.25 c., chopped)
- Firm tofu block (8 oz.)
- Garlic (2 cloves, diced)
- Grape tomatoes (0.5 c., halved)
- Kalamata olives (0.25 c., halved)
- Lemon juice (from ½ lemon)
- Nutritional yeast (2 Tbsp.)
- Olive oil (1 Tbsp.)
- Red bell pepper (0.5 c., chopped)
- Red onion (0.25, diced)
- Salt (pinch)
- Spinach (1 handful)
- Tahini paste (1 tsp)
- Salt and pepper to personal preference

Instructions

1. Break down tofu until the shape/texture of scrambled eggs. Then, combine in yeast, lemon juice, and tahini. Sprinkle with a pinch of salt.
2. Prepare skillet at a moderate heat. Sauté onions for 5 minutes before tossing in the pepper and garlic for an additional 5 minutes.
3. Mix in tofu and Kalamata olives. Warm through.
4. Toss in greens until wilted and reduced. Take off from heat and toss in tomatoes and season with salt and pepper to taste.

-

PART III

Keto Recipes

The keto diet is a high-fat and low-carb diet that comes with various health benefits. It has been found that this diet can help you lose weight and improve the condition of your health. It might also show some positive effects on cancer, diabetes, Alzheimer's, and epilepsy. This diet's main aim is to reduce the intake of carbs drastically and replace the same with healthy fats. When you reduce the consumption of carbs, the body will enter a metabolic state known as ketosis. During ketosis, the body will try its best to burn the body fat for generating energy. It will also be turning the liver fat into ketones that supply energy to the brain.

A keto diet is a very effective way of losing weight. The best aspect of this diet is that you can lose bodyweight without counting calories. The reason behind this is that the diet will be so filling that you will not have frequent cravings. It has been found that people who follow a keto diet can lose 2.5 times more weight when compared to those people who follow a calorie-restrictive diet. The keto diet can also deal with type 2 diabetes, metabolic, and prediabetes syndrome. Some other benefits of the keto diet are:

- **Cancer:** This diet can help suppress the growth of tumors and might also help in treating various types of cancer.

- **Heart diseases:** The keto diet can help deal with various chronic heart conditions such as heart attack, stroke, and others.

- **Polycystic ovary:**This diet is well known for reducing insulin levels that can help in dealing with polycystic ovary.

There are certain food items that you will need to include while following this diet.

- **Fatty fish**: Trout, salmon, mackerel, tuna

- **Meat**: Steak, sausage, red meat, ham, chicken, bacon, turkey

- **Seeds and nuts**: Walnuts, almonds, pumpkin seeds, flax seeds, chia seeds

- **Oils**: Coconut oil, olive oil, avocado oil

A keto diet is an excellent option for all those who have diabetes, overweight or want to improve the health of their metabolism. I have included some tasty and easy keto recipes that you can include in your diet plan.

Chapter 1: Gourmet Recipes

If you are looking for some tasty keto gourmet recipes, this section has got what you are searching for. So, let's have a look at them.

Creamy Garlic Chicken

Total Prep & Cooking Time: Twenty-five minutes

Yields: Six servings

Nutrition Facts: Calories: 348 | Protein: 28g | Carbs: 6.3g | Fat: 22.3g | Fiber: 0.9g

Ingredients

- Two pounds of chicken breasts (sliced thinly)
- Two tbsps. of olive oil
- One cup of each
    - Heavy cream
    - Spinach (chopped)
- Half cup of each
    - Chicken stock
    - Parmesan cheese
    - Sun-dried tomatoes
- One tsp. of each
    - Italian seasoning
    - Garlic powder

Method:

1. Take an iron skillet and add olive oil in it. After the oil gets hot, add the chicken and cook for five minutes. Remove the pieces of chicken from the skillet. Keep aside.

2. Add chicken stock, heavy cream, Italian seasoning, garlic powder, and parmesan cheese in the skillet. Whisk the mixture on medium flame until the sauce thickens. Add tomatoes and spinach. Simmer the mixture for two minutes until the spinach wilts.

3. Addcooked chicken into the prepared sauce. Cook for two minutes.

4. Serve hot.

Mediterranean Lemon Herb Chicken Salad

Total Prep & Cooking Time: Twenty-five minutes

Yields: Four servings

Nutrition Facts: Calories: 326 | Protein: 22.3g | Carbs: 12g | Fat: 20.1g | Fiber: 6.2g

Ingredients

- Two tbsps. of each
    - Olive oil
    - Water
    - Parsley (chopped)
    - Red wine vinegar
    - Basil (dried)
    - Garlic (minced)
- One lemon (juiced)
- One tsp. of each
    - Salt
    - Oregano
- One pound of chicken thighs

For the salad:

- Four cups of lettuce leaves (washed)
- One cucumber (diced)
- Two tomatoes (diced)
- One onion (sliced)
- One avocado (sliced)
- One-third cup of kalamata olives (sliced)
- Wedges of lemon (for serving)

Method:

1. Whisk all the marinade ingredients in a bowl. Pour half of the marinade in a shallow dish. Store the remaining marinade for the dressing.

2. Add the pieces of chicken in the marinade dish and marinate for half an hour.

3. Mix all the ingredients for the salad in a mixing bowl and keep aside.

4. Heat some oil in a grill pan. Add the marinated chicken and cook for five minutes on each side until browned on all sides.

5. Slice the chicken pieces.

6. Serve the salad with chicken from the top. Drizzle some of the marinade and serve with lemon wedges.

Garlic Butter Scallops and Steak

Total Prep & Cooking Time: Thirty minutes

Yields: Two servings

Nutrition Facts: Calories: 280 | Protein: 23.1g | Carbs: 1.2g | Fat: 1.3g | Fiber: 0.3g

Ingredients

- Two fillets of beef tenderloin
- Black pepper and kosher salt (according to taste)
- Three tbsps. of butter
- Ten sea scallops

For the sauce:

- Three garlic cloves (minced)
- Six tbsps. of butter (cubed)
- Two tbsps. of each
  - Chives (chopped)
  - Parsley (chopped)
- One tbsp. of lemon juice
- Two tsps. of lemon zest

- Black pepper and kosher salt (according to taste)

Method:

1. Take an iron skillet and heat it over medium flame for ten minutes.

2. Season the steak with pepper and salt.

3. Add two tbsps. of butter in the skillet. Add the steak and cook for six minutes on each side. Cook until the steak reaches your desired doneness.

4. Keep the steak aside and heat one tbsp. of butter in the skillet.

5. Remove the muscles from the small side of the scallops and wash them with cold running water.

6. Season the scallops with pepper and salt. Cook the scallops on each side for three minutes.

7. For making the sauce, add garlic and butter in a skillet. Stir for one minute. Add chives, lemon zest, parsley, and lemon juice. Add pepper and salt for seasoning.

8. Serve the scallops and steak with butter sauce from the top.

Fried Chicken

Total Prep & Cooking Time: Fifty minutes

Yields: Twelve servings

Nutrition Facts: Calories: 305 | Protein: 38.2g | Carbs: 0.6g | Fat: 12.3g | Fiber: 0.5g

Ingredients

- Four ounces of pork rinds
- Two tsps. of thyme (dried)

- One tsp. of each
    - Black pepper
    - Salt
    - Oregano (dried)
- Half tsp. of garlic powder
- One-third tsp. of paprika (smoked)
- Twelve chicken legs
- One large egg
- Two ounces of mayonnaise
- Three tbsps. of Dijon mustard

Method

1. Crush the pork rinds for making powder texture. Leave some of the big pieces.

2. Preheat the oven at 200 degrees Celsius.

3. Mix salt, pork rinds, thyme, pepper, garlic powder, oregano, and paprika. Spread out the prepared mixture on a large flat dish.

4. Combine Dijon mustard, egg, and mayonnaise in a bowl. Dip the chicken legs in the egg mixture and then roll in the mixture of pork rind. Coat well.

5. Place the legs of chicken on a baking tray. Bake for forty minutes.

6. Serve hot.

Lime Chile Steak Fajitas

Total Prep & Cooking Time: Twenty-five minutes

Yields: Four servings

Nutrition Facts: Calories: 419 | Protein: 23.1g | Carbs: 12g | Fat: 25.6g | Fiber: 5.1g

Ingredients

For the marinade:

- Two tbsps. of olive oil
- One-third cup of lime juice
- Three tbsps. of cilantro (chopped)
- Two garlic cloves (chopped)
- One tsp. of brown sugar
- Three-fourth tsp. of chili flakes
- Half tsp. of cumin (ground)
- One tsp. of salt
- One pound of steak

For the fajitas:

- Three capsicums (different colors, sliced)
- One avocado (sliced)
- One onion (sliced)

For serving:

- Tortillas
- Sour cream

Method:

1. Combine all the marinade ingredients in a bowl. Keep aside half of the marinade. Pour the remaining marinade in a flat dish and marinate the steak.

2. Heat one tsp. of oil in a skillet. Add the steak and grill for five minutes on each side. Allow the steak to cool down for five minutes.

3. Wipe the skillet and brush some oil. Fry the capsicums along with the strips of onion. Add the reserved marinade, pepper, and salt.

4. For serving the steak, slice the steak. Arrange steak, sour cream, avocado, and cooked veggies in the tortillas. Serve with marinade and cilantro from the top.

Spaghetti Squash With Stuffed Lasagna

Total Prep & Cooking Time: Two hours

Yields: Four servings

Nutrition Facts: Calories: 280 | Protein: 23.1g | Carbs: 6.7g | Fat: 21.3g | Fiber: 0.2g

Ingredients

- One pound of Italian sausage
- One spaghetti squash
- One cup of pasta sauce (low-carb)
- One-fourth cup of ricotta
- One-third cup of mozzarella
- Half cup of parmesan
- Pepper and salt (according to taste)
- Parsley (for garnishing)

Method:

1. Cut spaghetti squash in half. Remove the seeds. Bake the squash in the oven with the cut side down in one inch of water. Bake for fifty minutes at 200 degrees Celsius.

2. Take a skillet and add the sausage. Cook until browned and add pasta sauce. Simmer for ten minutes and add seasonings.

3. Take out the baked squash and scrape the inside portion with the help of a fork. Add the squash strands in a bowl.

4. Combine the strands with ricotta, meat sauce, and cheese.

5. Stuff the squash shells with the mixture and arrange in a baking sheet. Top with mozzarella.

6. Bake the squash for fifteen minutes until the cheese melts.

7. Serve with parsley from the top.

Total Prep & Cooking Time: Thirty minutes

Yields: Two servings

Nutrition Facts: Calories: 412 | Protein: 37.2g | Carbs: 23.2g | Fat: 18.3g | Fiber: 10.6g

Ingredients

- Two tsps. of avocado oil
- Half red bell pepper (diced)
- Two cans of wild tuna
- Half cup of salsa
- Two zucchinis
- Pepper and salt
- Half tsp. of cumin

For salsa:

- One avocado (cubed)
- One-fourth cup of cilantro (chopped)
- Three tbsps. of onion (minced)
- Two tsps. of lime juice

Method:

1. Take a frying pan and heat oil in it. Add diced pepper and sauté for two minutes. Remove the pepper and add tuna. Cook for four minutes.

2. Add salsa to the pan. Combine well.

3. Trim the zucchini ends. Slice them in half, lengthwise. Use a spoon for scraping out the flesh. Sprinkle some cumin, pepper, and salt.

4. Fill the zucchini shells with tuna mixture.

5. Preheat your oven at 200 degrees Celsius.

6. Bake the zucchini for twenty minutes.

7. Mix the ingredients for the salsa in a large small mixing bowl.

8. Serve the zucchini boats with salsa by the side.

Spinach and Goat Cheese Stuffed Breast of Chicken

Total Prep & Cooking Time: Forty-five minutes

Yields: Four servings

Nutrition Facts: Calories: 229 | Protein: 27.8g | Carbs: 4.9g | Fat: 13.7g | Fiber: 2.8g

Ingredients

- Four breasts of chicken
- Two tbsps. of olive oil
- Four cups of spinach
- Half tsp. of garlic powder
- Two ounces of goat cheese
- One onion (sliced)
- Eight ounces of bella mushrooms
- One tsp. of thyme
- Pepper and salt (for seasoning)

Method:

1. Heat the oven at 175 degrees Celsius.

2. Use a sharp knife for cutting slits on the upper side of the chicken breasts. Drizzle the breasts with olive oil, pepper, and salt. Keep aside.

3. Take a large skillet and heat half tbsp. of oil in it. Add spinach and cook for two minutes. Add garlic powder and cook until the spinach wilts.

4. Transfer spinach to a bowl. Add the goat cheese. Combine well.

5. Stuff the slits of the chicken breasts with the cheese and spinach mixture.

6. Heat one tbsp. of oil in the same skillet. Add mushrooms, onion, and thyme. Season with pepper and salt. Cook until the onions caramelize. Move the cooked veggies to a side to make some room for the chicken breasts.

7. Add the stuffed chicken breasts to the skillet.

8. Put the skillet in the oven. Bake for thirty minutes.

9. Serve hot.

Chapter 2: Quick and Easy Recipes

When you are short of time, opting for quick and easy recipes is the best option. So, I have included some easy recipes in this section that you can make without any hassle.

Antipasto Salad

Total Prep & Cooking Time: Thirty minutes

Yields: Two servings

Nutrition Facts: Calories: 510 | Protein: 36.8g | Carbs: 12.4g | Fat: 61g | Fiber: 10.6g

Ingredients

- Ten ounces of lettuce (chopped in pieces)
- Two tbsps. of parsley (chopped)
- Five ounces of mozzarella cheese (sliced)
- Three ounces of each
    - Salami (sliced thinly)
    - Prosciutto (sliced thinly)
- Four ounces of canned artichokes (quartered)
- Two cups of roasted red pepper
- One ounce of each
    - Sun-dried tomatoes (chopped)
    - Olives (sliced)
- One-third cup of basil

- One chili pepper (chopped)
- Half tbsp. of salt
- Four tbsps. of olive oil

Method:

1. Distribute the leaves of lettuce on serving plates or on a large dish.

2. Add parsley from the top.

3. Layer all the ingredients of antipasto.

4. In a bowl, mix chopped chili, basil, and salt. Crush the ingredients using a wooden spoon.

5. Sprinkle the crushed mixture over the salad and serve with olive oil from the top.

Feta Cheese and Chicken Plate
Total Prep & Cooking Time: Ten minutes

Yields: Two servings

Nutrition Facts: Calories: 810 | Protein: 63.3g | Carbs: 8.7g | Fat: 71g | Fiber: 3.2g

Ingredients

- Five-hundred grams of rotisserie chicken
- Two cups of feta cheese
- Two tomatoes
- Three cups of lettuce
- Ten olives
- One-third cup of olive oil
- Pepper and salt (according to taste)

Method:

1. Arrange chicken, lettuce, cheese, and olives on a plate. Slice the tomatoes and arrange them on the plate.

2. Sprinkle pepper and salt for seasoning.

3. Serve with olive oil from the top.

Note: If you do not want to use rotisserie chicken, you can cook the chicken from scratch.

Cheese Omelet

Total Prep & Cooking Time: Fifteen minutes

Yields: Two servings

Nutrition Facts: Calories: 797 | Protein: 37.2g | Carbs: 3.9g | Fat: 74.2g | Fiber: 0.1g

Ingredients

- Half cup of butter
- Six large eggs
- One cup of cheddar cheese (shredded)
- Pepper and salt (according to taste)

Method:

1. Break the eggs in a bowl. Add the cheese and whisk. Season with pepper and salt.

2. Take a medium-sized pan and melt some butter in it. Add the whisked egg mixture and allow it to set for two minutes.

3. Reduce the flame and cook for four minutes on each side. Add the leftover cheese.

4. Fold the omelet in half. Cook for one more minute.

5. Serve hot.

Baked Salmon and Pesto

Total Prep & Cooking Time: Thirty minutes

Yields: Four servings

Nutrition Facts: Calories: 625 | Protein: 48.3g | Carbs: 3.2g | Fat: 89g | Fiber: 0.7g

Ingredients

- Four tbsps. of pesto
- One cup of mayonnaise
- Half cup of Greek yogurt
- Pepper and salt (according to taste)

For the salmon:

- Four fillets of salmon
- Four tbsps. of green pesto
- Pepper and salt (for seasoning)

Method:

1. Grease a baking dish with some oil. Place the fillets of salmon on the dish with the skin-side down. Spread green pesto on the fillets and season with pepper and salt.

2. Bake the salmon for thirty minutes at 200 degrees Celsius.

3. Stir the ingredients for the sauce in a bowl.

4. Serve the salmon with sauce from the top.

Pork Chops and Blue Cheese Sauce

Total Prep & Cooking Time: Twenty minutes

Yields: Four servings

Nutrition Facts: Calories: 669 | Protein: 53.2g | Carbs: 4.3g | Fat: 60.1g | Fiber: 1.6g

Ingredients

- Two cups of blue cheese
- One cup of whipping cream (heavy)
- Four pork chops
- Seven ounces of green beans
- Two tbsps. of butter
- Pepper and salt

Method:

1. Crumble the blue cheese in a pot. Place the pot over medium flame and allow the cheese to melt.

2. Add whipping cream in the melted cheese and mix well. Simmer for two minutes.

3. Season the chops using pepper and salt.

4. Take an iron skillet and heat some oil in it. Add the chops and cook for four minutes on each side.

5. Add the juices from the pan in the sauce and stir.

6. Trim the beans. Heat some oil butter in the skillet and sauté the beans for two minutes.

7. Serve the pork chops with cheese sauce from the top and beans by the side.

Green Pepper and Pork Stir-Fry

Total Prep & Cooking Time: Twenty-five minutes

Yields: Two servings

Nutrition Facts: Calories: 678 | Protein: 31.2g | Carbs: 5.3g | Fat: 71.3g | Fiber: 4.6g

Ingredients

- Four ounces of butter
- Four-hundred grams of pork shoulder (cut in strips)
- Two bell pepper (green, sliced)
- Two scallions (sliced)
- Half cup of almond
- One tsp. of chili paste
- Pepper and salt

Method:

1. Heat butter in a wok. Add the meat strips in the butter and cook for five minutes until browned.

2. Add the chili paste along with veggies. Cook for two minutes. Add pepper and salt.

3. Serve the stir-fry with almonds from the top.

Broccoli With Fried Chicken

Total Prep & Cooking Time: Thirty minutes

Yields: Two servings

Nutrition Facts: Calories: 633 | Protein: 30.1g | Carbs: 5.3g | Fat: 64.3g | Fiber: 3.6g

Ingredients

- Nine ounces of broccoli
- One cup of butter
- Ten ounces of chicken thighs (boneless)
- Pepper and salt
- Half cup of mayonnaise

Method:

1. Rinse the broccoli thoroughly under running water. Trim the florets along with the stem.

2. Heat some butter in a pan.

3. Season the chicken thighs. Add the chicken to the pan and cook them for five minutes on all sides.

4. Add some more butter in the pan and add the broccoli. Toss the broccoli and chicken and cook for two minutes.

5. Serve with mayonnaise from the top.

Fried Eggs With Pork and Kale
Total Prep & Cooking Time: Twenty-five minutes

Yields: Three servings

Nutrition Facts: Calories: 910 | Protein: 24g | Carbs: 7.6g | Fat: 89g | Fiber: 6.3g

Ingredients

- One cup of kale
- Three ounces of butter
- Six ounces of bacon or pork belly (smoked)
- One ounce of walnuts
- Four large eggs
- Pepper and salt

Method:

1. Chop the kale and wash them under cold water.

2. Melt some butter in a skillet and cook the kale for two minutes until the edges are slightly browned.

3. Remove kale from the skillet and keep aside. Add bacon or pork belly in the same skillet and sear until crispy.

4. Add the kale in the skillet along with walnuts. Toss the ingredients.

5. Heat butter in another pan and fry the eggs sunny side up. Add pepper and salt for seasoning.

6. Serve the eggs with kale mixture by the side.

Chapter 3: Sweet Recipes

Even when you are on a diet, you don't have to compromise on satisfying your sweet tooth. So, I have included some easy to make sweet keto recipes in this section.

Sugar Cinnamon Donuts

Total Prep & Cooking Time: Twenty-five minutes

Yields: Twelve servings

Nutrition Facts: Calories: 82 | Protein: 2.3g | Carbs: 1.9g | Fat: 7.8g | Fiber: 0.3g

Ingredients

- Two eggs
- One-fourth cup of almond milk
- One-fourth tsp. of apple cider vinegar
- One tsp. of vanilla extract

- Two tbsps. of butter
- One-third cup of sweetener
- One cup of fine almond flour
- Half tbsp. of coconut flour
- One tsp. of cinnamon (ground)
- One and a half tsp. of baking powder
- Half tsp. of baking soda
- Half cup of salt

For sugar cinnamon coating:

- One-fourth cup of granulated erythritol
- One tsp. of cinnamon (ground)
- Two tbsps. of butter

Method:

1. Whisk together almond milk, eggs, butter, vinegar, vanilla extract, and sweetener. Combine until smooth.

2. Combine coconut flour, almond flour, baking powder, cinnamon, salt, and baking soda in a bowl. Add all the dry ingredients slowly to the mixture of wet ingredients. Stir well until combined.

3. Transfer the donut batter into a donut pan.

4. Bake the donuts for fifteen minutes at 175 degrees Celsius.

5. Take out the donuts and keep aside for cooling.

6. Stir together cinnamon and sweetener in a bowl.

7. Melt the butter in a pan.

8. Take the donuts and dunk them in the butter. Roll the donuts in the cinnamon coating.

Mug Brownie

Total Prep & Cooking Time: Ten minutes

Yields: Two servings

Nutrition Facts: Calories: 194 | Protein: 7.9g | Carbs: 7.6g | Fat: 16.5g | Fiber: 6.7g

Ingredients

- Two tbsps. of almond flour
- One tbsp. of each
  - Granulated sweetener
  - Cocoa powder
  - Almond butter
  - Chocolate chips
- One-eighth tsp. of baking powder
- Three tbsps. of milk

Method:

1. Use a cooking spray for greasing cereal bowls or mugs.

2. Combine the listed dry ingredients. Mix properly.

3. Mix milk and almond butter in a separate bowl and mix well.

4. Combine the dry and wet ingredients. Mix well. Add the chocolate chips and fold well.

5. Pour the batter in the cereal bowls. Bake for six minutes.

6. Enjoy your brownie from the bowl.

Mini Cheesecake

Total Prep & Cooking Time: Three hours and twenty minutes

Yields: Six servings

Nutrition Facts: Calories: 230 | Protein: 4.7g | Carbs: 5.1g | Fat: 19.6g | Fiber: 1.8g

Ingredients

For the crust:

- Half cup of almond flour
- Two tbsps. of sweetener
- Half tsp. of cinnamon
- Two tbsps. of butter (melted)

For the filling:

- Six ounces of cream cheese (softened)
- Five tbsps. of sweetener
- One-fourth cup of sour cream
- Half tsp. of vanilla extract
- One egg
- Two tsps. of cinnamon (ground)

For the frosting:

- One tbsp. of butter (softened)
- Three tbsps. of confectioners sweetener
- One-fourth tsp. of vanilla extract
- Two tsps. of heavy cream

Method:

1. Heat the oven at 175 degrees Celsius. Line a small muffin pan with six silicone liners.

2. Whisk almond flour, cinnamon, and sweetener in a bowl. Add melted butter and mix well.

3. Divide the prepared crust among the muffin cups. Press the crust to the bottom. Bake in the oven for five minutes.

4. Beat three tbsps. of sweetener along with the cream cheese in a bowl. Add vanilla, egg, and sour cream. Beat well.

5. Reduce oven temperature to 160 degrees Celsius.

6. Whisk cinnamon and butter in a bowl.

7. Add three-fourth tbsp. of cheese mixture into the muffin cups. Sprinkle cinnamon mixture from the top.

8. Bake the muffins for fifteen minutes. Refrigerate the muffins for two hours.

9. Beat powdered sweetener and butter in a bowl. Add heavy cream and vanilla extract. Mix well.

10. Transfer the frosting to a zip-lock bag and cut a small hole at the corner.

11. Add frosting over the cheesecakes.

Keto Fudge

Total Prep & Cooking Time: One hour

Yields: Twelve servings

Nutrition Facts: Calories: 158 | Protein: 0.1g | Carbs: 0.6g | Fat: 17.9g | Fiber: 0.7g

Ingredients

- One cup of coconut oil
- One-fourth cup of each
  - Cocoa powder
  - Erythritol (powdered)
- One tsp. of vanilla extract
- One-eighth tsp. of sea salt
- Sea salt

Method:

1. Use parchment paper for lining a glass baking dish.

2. Beat sweetener and coconut oil using a hand blender. Make sure the mixture is fluffy.

3. Add vanilla extract, cocoa powder, and salt. Combine well.

4. Pour the fudge mixture in the lined dish. Smoothen the top using a spoon or spatula.

5. Refrigerate the fudge for forty minutes until it solidifies.

6. Use a sharp knife to run along the edges of the dish for taking out the fudge.

7. Cut in small cubes and serve.

Peanut Butter Hearts

Total Prep & Cooking Time: Thirty minutes

Yields: Twenty servings

Nutrition Facts: Calories: 91 | Protein: 5.1g | Carbs: 7.1g | Fat: 6.7g | Fiber: 5.2g

Ingredients

- Two cups of peanut butter
- Three-fourth cup of any sticky sweetener
- One cup of coconut flour
- One and a half cup of chocolate chips

Method:

1. Use parchment paper for lining a large glass tray.

2. Combine sticky sweetener with peanut butter on the stovetop. Combine the mixture until it melts completely.

3. Add the coconut flour and combine. In case the batter is very thin, you can add more flour.

4. Make twenty balls from the dough. Use a heart-shaped cookie cutter for pressing the dough balls for making heart shape.

5. Arrange the hearts on the lined glass tray and refrigerate.

6. Melt the chocolate chips and dip the hearts in the melted chocolate.

7. Refrigerate again for twenty minutes until firm.

Peanut Butter and White Chocolate Blondies

Total Prep & Cooking Time: Three hours and thirty-five minutes

Yields: Sixteen servings

Nutrition Facts: Calories: 102 | Protein: 3.2g | Carbs: 2.2g | Fat: 9.3g | Fiber: 1.9g

Ingredients

- Half cup of each
    - Peanut butter
    - Sweetener of your choice
- Four tbsps. of butter (softened)
- Two large eggs
- One tsp. of vanilla extract
- Three tbsps. of cocoa butter (melted)
- One-fourth cup of almond flour
- One tbsp. of coconut flour
- One cup of cocoa butter (chopped)

Method:

1. Heat the oven at 175 degrees Celsius. Use a cooking spray for greasing a baking dish.

2. Combine all the ingredients in a large bowl using a hand mixer.

3. Pour the mixture in the greased dish.

4. Bake for thirty minutes.

5. Cool the blondies and refrigerate for about three hours.

6. Cut the blondies in squares and serve.

Low Carb Ice Cream

Total Prep & Cooking Time: Five hours and thirty-five minutes

Yields: Eight servings

Nutrition Facts: Calories: 337 | Protein: 2.2g | Carbs: 3.1g | Fat: 34g | Fiber: 0.3g

Ingredients

- Three tbsps. of butter
- Three cups of heavy cream
- One-third cup of powdered allulose
- One-fourth cup of coconut oil
- One tsp. of vanilla extract
- One medium-sized bean of vanilla

Method:

1. Take a pan and heat it over medium flame. Melt butter in it. Add a two-third cup of the heavy cream along with sweetener. Boil the mixture and simmer for thirty minutes.

2. Pour the mixture in a bowl and let it cool at room temperature. Add vanilla seeds from the bean along with the vanilla extract. Add coconut oil and mix well.

3. Add the remaining cream and combine until smooth.

4. Pour the mixture in a container and use a spatula for smoothening the top.

5. Freeze the ice cream for five hours. Ensure that you stir the ice cream mixture after every thirty minutes for the first two hours and then after every sixty minutes.

Chocolate Donut

Total Prep & Cooking Time: One hour and twenty-five minutes

Yields: Ten servings

Nutrition Facts: Calories: 219 | Protein: 5.1g | Carbs: 7.6g | Fat: 18.6g | Fiber: 3.1g

Ingredients

- Four eggs
- Half cup of butter (melted)
- Three tbsps. of milk
- One tsp. of stevia
- One-fourth cup of each
  o Coconut flour
  o Cocoa powder (unsweetened)
  o Sea salt
  o Baking soda

For the glaze:

- One tbsp. of avocado oil
- Three-fourth cup of chocolate chips

Method:

1. Heat the oven at 175 degrees Celsius.

2. Use a cooking spray for greasing donut pan of ten cavities.

3. Mix melted butter, eggs, and stevia, and milk in a bowl.

4. Add cocoa powder, coconut flour, baking soda, and salt.

5. Pour the mixture in the donut pan. Bake the donuts for fifteen minutes until set.

6. Let the donuts cool for fifteen minutes.

7. Add the chocolate chips in a bowl and melt in the microwave. Add avocado oil and stir.

8. Take out the donuts and dip them in the chocolate glaze.

9. Let the donuts sit for thirty minutes.

Chapter 4: Savory Recipes

In this section, I have included some tasty savory keto recipes that you can enjoy at any time of the day. So, let's have a look at them.

Keto McMuffin

Total Prep & Cooking Time: Twenty minutes

Yields: Two servings

Nutrition Facts: Calories: 610 | Protein: 24g | Carbs: 3.2g | Fat: 51.8g | Fiber: 6.9g

Ingredients

- One-fourth cup of each
  - o   Almond flour
  - o   Flaxmeal
- One-fourth tsp. of baking soda
- One egg
- Two tbsps. of heavy whipping cream
- One cup of cheddar cheese (shredded)
- Three tbsps. of water
- Salt (for seasoning)

For the filling:

- Two large eggs
- One tbsp. of butter
- Two cheddar cheese slices
- One tsp. of Dijon mustard
- Pepper and salt (for seasoning)

Method:

1. Combine all the dry ingredients. Mix well.

2. Add cream, water, and egg. Combine well using a fork.

3. Add the shredded cheese and mix.

4. Pour the mixture in greased ramekins. Microwave the mixture at high settings for two minutes.

5. Take a pan and fry the eggs. Add pepper and salt for seasoning.

6. Cut the prepared muffins in half. Spread butter on the inside portion of the muffin halves.

7. Top the muffin slices with egg, cheese, and mustard.

8. Serve immediately.

Sausage Hash With Rainbow Chard

Total Prep & Cooking Time: Twenty-five minutes

Yields: Two servings

Nutrition Facts: Calories: 570 | Protein: 25g | Carbs: 7.6g | Fat: 44.6g | Fiber: 5.6g

Ingredients

- Two-hundred grams of Swiss chard
- Two cups of cauliflower rice
- One-hundred and fifty grams of sausage meat
- Three tbsps. of lard
- Two garlic cloves (chopped)
- One tbsp. of lemon juice
- One tsp. of Dijon mustard
- Pepper and salt
- Four poached eggs

Method:

1. Chop the chard stalks into small pieces.

2. Take a greased skillet and add the sausage meat. Cook for five minutes until browned. Keep aside

3. Add the remaining lard to the same skillet. Add the garlic. Cook for one minute and add the cauliflower rice. Cook the mixture for five minutes.

4. Add the chard and Dijon mustard. Combine well. Add lemon juice and cook the mixture for two minutes. Add pepper and salt for seasoning.

5. Add the sausage meat and mix.

6. Serve with poached eggs.

Veggie and Chicken Sausage Skillet

Total Prep & Cooking Time: Thirty minutes

Yields: Four servings

Nutrition Facts: Calories: 310 | Protein: 21g | Carbs: 9.3g | Fat: 22.3g | Fiber: 2.4g

Ingredients

- Three tbsps. of butter
- Five links of chicken sausage (sliced)
- Two garlic cloves (minced)
- One red onion (cut in chunks)
- One zucchini (sliced in rounds)
- One summer squash (sliced in rounds)
- One red capsicum (cut in chunks)
- One yellow capsicum (cut in chunks)
- Six cremini mushrooms (quartered)
- Half tsp. of each
  - Red pepper flakes (crushed)
  - Italian seasoning
- Pepper and salt

Method:

1. Take an iron skillet and melt some butter in it.

2. Add the sausage, onion, and garlic. Sauté the mixture for ten minutes.

3. Add the veggies and mix well. Add pepper flakes, Italian seasoning, pepper, and salt.

4. Sauté the mixture for fifteen minutes and serve hot.

Total Prep & Cooking Time: Twenty-five minutes

Yields: Ten servings

Nutrition Facts: Calories: 37 | Protein: 2.3g | Carbs: 1.3g | Fat: 2.7g | Fiber: 6.3g

Ingredients

- Two ounces of dried salami
- One ounce of cream cheese
- Half cup of parsley (chopped)

Method:

1. Heat the oven at 170 degrees Celsius.

2. Slice the salami into thirty slices of a quarter inch.

3. Arrange the salami on a baking pan.

4. Bake them for fifteen minutes.

5. Top the salami with cream cheese along with parsley.

Buffalo Chicken Sandwich

Total Prep & Cooking Time: Twenty-five minutes

Yields: Four servings

Nutrition Facts: Calories: 480 | Protein: 27g | Carbs: 5.1g | Fat: 30g | Fiber: 2.2g

Ingredients

- Two cups of cooked chicken (shredded)
- One-third cup of red pepper sauce
- Three tbsps. of butter
- One-fourth tsp. of each
  - Celery seed spice
  - Sea salt
  - Garlic powder
- Two tbsps. of each
  - Blue cheese crumbles
  - Celery (minced)
- Four tbsps. of ranch dressing
- Three tbsps. of mayonnaise
- Four sandwich buns

Method:

1. Take a medium saucepan and melt butter in it. Add celery seed spice, red pepper sauce, sea salt, and garlic powder. Stir well.

2. Add the chicken along with celery to the pan. Mix well and cook for two minutes.

3. Add the mayonnaise and combine.

4. Cut the buns in half. Add half cup of prepared chicken mixture on the buns. Top the chicken with one tbsp. of ranch dressing and half tbsp. of cheese crumbles.

5. Place the other halves on top and serve.

Cream Cheese and Salmon Bites
Total Prep & Cooking Time: Twenty minutes

Yields: Ten servings

Nutrition Facts: Calories: 43 | Protein: 1.3g | Carbs: 0.3g | Fat: 4.6g | Fiber: 0.6g

Ingredients

- Two eggs
- Half cup of cream
- One tbsp. of salt
- One cup of cheese (shredded)
- One-third tsp. of dill (dried)
- One-third cup of cream cheese (diced)
- Two cups of salmon (smoked, chopped)

Method:

1. Combine cream, eggs, and salt in a bowl.

2. Add cheese, cream cheese, and dill. Mix well.

3. Grease a muffin tray with butter.

4. Pour the mixture in the muffin tray. Add some pieces of salmon into each muffin.

5. Bake the mixture in the oven for twenty minutes at 180 degrees Celsius.

6. Remove the bites and serve warm.Vegetable Turkey Pesto Bolognese

Total Prep & Cooking Time: Thirty minutes

Yields: Four servings

Nutrition Facts: Calories: 270 | Protein: 20.1g | Carbs: 4.3g | Fat: 13.2g | Fiber: 1.6g

Ingredients

- Two tsps. of oil
- One pound of turkey (ground)
- One cup of onion (diced)
- Two cups of each
    - Mushrooms (sliced)
    - Zucchini (sliced)
- Three tbsps. of pesto sauce
- Pasta of your choice (cooked)
- Grated cheese

Method:

1. Take a large skillet and add some oil. Add the turkey and cook until browned. Keep aside.

2. Add onions in the same and cook for two minutes. Add mushrooms and zucchini. Mix well.

3. Add the cooked turkey and combine it. Add pesto sauce simmer for five minutes.

4. Add cooked pasta along with cheese. Stir to combine. Simmer for two minutes.

5. Serve hot.

Turkey Patties

Total Prep & Cooking Time: Thirty minutes

Yields: Four servings

Nutrition Facts: Calories: 435 | Protein: 24g | Carbs: 4.5g | Fat: 37.2g | Fiber: 2.5g

Ingredients

- Five-hundred grams of ground turkey
- Half cup of almond flour
- One hot chili pepper (finely chopped)
- Two tsps. of Dijon mustard
- Two tbsps. of each
    o Parsley (chopped)
    o Lemon juice
    o Basil (chopped)
- Half tsp. of sea salt
- One tsp. black pepper (ground)
- Two spring onions (sliced finely)
- Two tbsps. of lard
- One egg
- Two garlic cloves (crushed)

Method:

1. Combine turkey, eggs, almond flour, garlic, pepper, lemon juice, Dijon mustard, basil, parsley, black pepper, and salt. Add the spring onions and mix well.

2. Make small patties using your hands.

3. Heat lard in a pan and add the patties. Cook the patties for five minutes on each side.

4. Let the patties sit for two minutes. Serve warm with spring onions.

Chapter 5: Poultry and Meat Recipes

Meat and poultry are rich in protein and various other nutrients that you need for perfect health. In this section, you will find some tasty poultry and meat keto recipes that you can make at home.

Beef Cabbage Skillet

Total Prep & Cooking Time: Thirty minutes

Yields: Four servings

Nutrition Facts: Calories: 357 | Protein: 13g | Carbs: 27g | Fat: 7.2g | Fiber: 11.3g

Ingredients

- Half green cabbage (shredded)
- Two tbsps. of butter
- One pound of beef (ground)
- Three tbsps. of taco seasoning
- One tsp. of minced onion (dried)
- One and a half cup of Mexican cheese blend
- Pepper and salt (according to taste)

Method:

1. Take a large skillet and heat one tbsp. of butter in it. Add shredded cabbage and sauté for two minutes. Keep aside.

2. Add one tbsp. of butter in the same skillet. Add the beef. Add onion, taco seasoning, and mix well. Cook for five minutes. Add one-fourth cup of water. Add the cooked cabbage along with pepper and salt. Combine half a cup of cheese.

3. Top with leftover cheese and place the skillet in the oven. Bake for ten minutes or until the cheese melts.

Meatball Casserole

Total Prep & Cooking Time: Three hours and thirty minutes

Yields: Six servings

Nutrition Facts: Calories: 470 | Protein: 37g | Carbs: 5.4g | Fat: 33.2g | Fiber: 4.7g

Ingredients

- Two pounds of beef (ground)
- Half cup of each
  - Mozzarella cheese
  - Parmesan cheese
- Two tbsps. of coconut flour
- Two large eggs
- Three-fourth tsp. of each
  - Onion (minced)
  - Salt
- One-fourth tsp. of Italian seasoning
- Half tsp. of garlic powder
- Twenty ounce can of spaghetti sauce
- Two cups of mozzarella cheese
- One tsp. of dried basil

Method:

1. Mix the ingredients in a bowl except for the spaghetti sauce, basil, and two cups of mozzarella cheese.

2. Heat a skillet on medium flame. Add one-fourth inch of coconut oil in the skillet.

3. Scoop meatballs from the mixture and add them to the skillet.

4. Cook the meatballs for five minutes until browned.

5. Place the meatballs in the base of a crockpot.

6. Add spaghetti sauce from the top.

7. Cook the meatballs on high for three hours.

8. Take out the meatballs in a baking dish.

9. Sprinkle cheese from the top.

10. Broil the meatballs for three minutes until cheese melts.

Beef Taquitos

Total Prep & Cooking Time: Forty minutes

Yields: Six servings

Nutrition Facts: Calories: 229 | Protein: 15.7g | Carbs: 1.6g | Fat: 16.3g | Fiber: 0.3g

Ingredients

- One cup of each
    o Cheddar cheese (shredded)
    o Mozzarella cheese (shredded)
- Half cup of parmesan cheese (grated)
- Half pound of beef (ground)
- One-fourth cup of onion (minced)
- Half tsp. of each
    o Paprika
    o Chili powder
    o Salt
    o Onion powder
    o Garlic powder
- One tsp. of cumin
- One-fourth tsp. of pepper
- One-third cup of water

Method:

1. Mix chili powder, cumin, garlic powder, onion powder, pepper, salt in a cup, and some water.

2. Take a skillet and brown the beef along with the onion. Add the mixture over the beef and simmer for ten minutes.

3. Mix all the cheese in a bowl. Divide the mixture of cheese for making six balls. Use parchment paper to line a baking sheet. Place them on the sheet and bake for eight minutes.

4. Let the cheese sheets cool down for two minutes.

5. Take one spoon of the beef mixture and place it on the edge of the cheese sheets. Repeat for the remaining sheets.

6. Roll them tightly for making cigar shape.

7. Serve warm.

Chicken Wings

Total Prep & Cooking Time: Fifty minutes

Yields: Four servings

Nutrition Facts: Calories: 287 | Protein: 2.3g | Carbs: 12g | Fat: 16.3g | Fiber: 1.9g

Ingredients

- Two pounds of chicken wings
- Two tsps. of salt
- Three-fourth cup of coconut aminos
- One-fourth tsp. of each

- o   Onion powder
- o   Ginger (ground)
- o   Garlic powder
- o   Chili flakes

Method:

1. Place the wings on a baking tray.

2. Sprinkle some salt evenly on the wings.

3. Bake the chicken wings in the oven for forty minutes at 180 degrees Celsius.

4. Take a skillet and add coconut aminos. Add garlic powder, ginger, onion powder, and chili flakes. Simmer the sauce and stir until the sauce thickens.

5. Place the cooked wings in a large bowl and pour the sauce over the wings. Toss the cooked wings in the prepared sauce. Coat evenly.

6. Serve hot.

Roasted Leg of Chicken

Total Prep & Cooking Time: One hour and ten minutes

Yields: Four servings

Nutrition Facts: Calories: 687 | Protein: 27.9g | Carbs: 10.1g | Fat: 58.9g | Fiber: 6g

Ingredients

- Four legs of chicken
- Four tbsps. of olive oil
- Two tbsps. of Italian seasoning
- Pepper and salt
- Twenty ounces of each
  - Cherry tomatoes
  - Broccoli

For the garlic butter:

- Four ounces of butter
- Two cloves of garlic (smashed)
- Pepper and salt

Method:

1. Toss the legs of the chicken with seasoning and oil.

2. Place the chicken legs in a baking sheet along with the tomatoes. Bake for forty-five minutes at 150 degrees Celsius.

3. As the chicken is cooking, cut the broccoli. Divide the florets and also slice the stem. Boil them in water for five minutes, along with some salt. Drain the broccoli water.

4. For making the garlic butter, combine all the ingredients in a small bowl.

5. Serve the cooked chicken legs with tomatoes, broccoli, and garlic butter by the side.

Note: Place the chicken legs in the oven with the skin side up.

Chapter 6: Staple Recipes

In this section, I have included some simple keto recipes made from everyday staples. Let's have a look at them.

Keto Waffles

Total Prep & Cooking Time: Ten minutes

Yields: Two servings

Nutrition Facts: Calories: 160 | Protein: 21.3g | Carbs: 12.6g | Fat: 5.6g | Fiber: 10.3g

Ingredients

- Four tbsps. of coconut flour
- One tbsp. of each
    - Granulated sweetener
    - Apple sauce (unsweetened)
- One-fourth tsp. of each
    - Baking powder
    - Cinnamon
- Two-third cup of egg whites
- One-fourth cup of milk
- Half tsp. of vanilla extract
- One tsp. of coconut oil

Method:

1. Take a mixing bowl and mix the dry ingredients. Keep aside.

2. Add egg whites, vanilla extract, milk, and apple sauce in a bowl. Pour this mixture into the mixture of dry ingredients. Mix well.

3. Heat a waffle iron and grease with cooking spray or oil.

4. Add the waffle batter and cook for five minutes until fluffy and crisp.

Cookie Dough

Total Prep & Cooking Time: Ten minutes

Yields: Four servings

Nutrition Facts: Calories: 130 | Protein: 4.6g | Carbs: 4.3g | Fat: 12g | Fiber: 2.9g

Ingredients

- Half cup of almond flour
- Two tbsps. of each
    - Sticky sweetener
    - Granulated sweetener
    - Coconut flour
- One and a half tbsp. of coconut oil
- One tbsp. of chocolate chips

Method:

1. Combine coconut flour, almond flour, and granulated sugar in a bowl.

2. Add coconut oil and sticky sweetener. Mix well. Add the chocolate chips.

3. You can either enjoy the dough immediately or refrigerate it for thirty minutes.

Baked Tofu

Total Prep & Cooking Time: One hour and ten minutes

Yields: Two servings

Nutrition Facts: Calories: 131.3 | Protein: 11.3g | Carbs: 3.1g | Fat: 8.6g | Fiber: 1.7g

Ingredients

- One block of tofu (firm)
- One tbsp. of each
  - Soy sauce
  - Sesame oil
  - Tamari
- Half tsp. of each
  - Ginger
  - Garlic powder
  - Cayenne powder

Method:

1. Mix all the listed ingredients except for the tofu. Let the marinade sit for five minutes.

2. Chop the block of tofu into small pieces. Add the tofu cubes in the marinade. Refrigerate for half an hour.

3. Use parchment paper for lining a baking tray. Add the marinated tofu and bake for thirty minutes. Flip the tofu cubes halfway.

4. Serve immediately.

Cauliflower Fried Rice

Total Prep & Cooking Time: Twenty minutes

Yields: Four servings

Nutrition Facts: Calories: 135 | Protein: 7.9g | Carbs: 10.3g | Fat: 7.6g | Fiber: 8.6g

Ingredients

- Two tbsps. of sesame oil
- Two garlic cloves (finely chopped)
- One onion (finely chopped)
- Two scallions
- One-fourth cup of carrots (finely chopped)
- Eight cups of cauliflower rice
- Half cup of soy sauce
- One-fourth tsp. of cayenne pepper

Method:

1. Take a large wok and heat it over a medium flame. Addsome oil in it. Add garlic and onion. Cook for two minutes. Add scallions and carrots. Sauté for two minutes.

2. Add the cauliflower rice and combine well. Add cayenne and soy sauce. Fry for four minutes.

3. Serve the fried rice with scallions from the top.

PART IV

Chapter 1: Meal Planning 101

Sticking to a diet is something that is not the easiest in the world. When it comes down to it, we struggle to change up our diets on a whim. It might be that for the first few days, you are able to stick to it and make sure that you are only eating those foods that are better for you, but over time, you will get to a point where you feel the pressure to cave in. You might realize that sticking to your diet is difficult and think that stopping for a burger on your way home won't be too bad. You might think that figuring out lunch or dinner is too much of a hassle, or you realize that the foods that you have bought forgot a key ingredient that you needed for dinner.

The good news is, you have an easy fix. When you are able to figure out what you are making for yourself for your meals well in advance, you stop having to worry so much about the foods that you eat, what you do with them, and what you are going to reach for when it's time to eat. You will be able to change up what you are doing so that you can be certain that the meals that you are enjoying are good for you, and you won't have to worry so much about the stress that goes into it. Let's take a look at what you need to do to get started with meal planning so that you can begin to do so without having to think too much about it.

Make a Menu

First, before you do anything, make sure that you make a menu! This should be something that you do on your own, or you should sit down with your family to ask them what they prefer. If you can do this, you will be able to ensure that you've got a clear-cut plan. When you have a menu a week in advance, you save yourself time and money because you know that all of your meals will use ingredients that are similar, and you won't have to spend forever thinking about what you should make at any point in time.

Plan around Ads

When you do your menu, make it a point to glance through the weekly ads as well. Typically, you will find that there are plenty of deals that you can make use of that will save you money.

Go Meatless Once Per Week

A great thing to do that is highly recommended on the Mediterranean Diet is to have a day each week where you go meatless for dinner. By doing so, you will realize that you can actually cut costs and enjoy the foods more at the same time. It is a great way to get that additional fruit and veggie content into your day, and there are plenty of healthy options that are out there for you. You just have to commit to doing so. In the meal plans that you'll see below, you will notice that there will be a meatless day on Day 2 every week.

Use Ingredients That You Already Have On Hand

Make it a point to use ingredients that you already have on hand whenever possible. Alternatively, make sure that all of the meals that you eat during the week use very similar ingredients. When you do this, you know that you're avoiding causing any waste or losing ingredients along the way, meaning that you can save money. The good news is, on the Mediterranean diet, there are plenty of delicious meals that enjoy very similar ingredients that you can eat.

Avoid Recipes that Call for a Special Ingredient

If you're trying to avoid waste, it is a good idea for you to avoid any ingredients in meals that are not going to carry over to other meals during your weekly plan. By avoiding doing so, you can usually save yourself that money for that one ingredient that would be wasted. Alternatively, if you find that you really want that dish, try seeing if you can freeze some of it for later. When you do that, you can usually ensure that your special ingredient at least didn't go to waste.

Use Seasonal Foods

Fruits and veggies are usually cheaper when you buy them in season, and even better, when you do so, you will be enjoying a basic factor of the Mediterranean diet just by virtue of enjoying the foods when they are fresh. Fresher foods are usually tastier, and they also tend to carry more vitamins and minerals because they have not had the chance to degrade over time.

Make Use of Leftovers and Extra Portions

One of the greatest things that you can do when it comes to meal planning is to make use of your leftovers and make-ahead meals. When you do this regularly, making larger portions than you need, you can then use the extras as lunches and dinners all week long, meaning that you won't have to be constantly worrying about the food that you eat for lunch. We will use some of these in the meal plans that you will see as well.

Eat What You Enjoy

Finally, the last thing to remember with your meal plan is that you ought to be enjoying the foods that are on it at all times. When you ensure that the foods that you have on your plate are those that you actually enjoy, sticking to your meal plan doesn't become such a chore, and that means that you will be able to do better as well with your own diet. Your meal plan should be loaded up with foods that you are actually excited about enjoying. Meal planning and dieting should not be a drag—you should love every moment of it!

Chapter 2: 1 Month Meal Plan

This meal plan is designed to be used for one month to help you simplify making sure that you have delicious meals to eat without having to think. These meals are fantastic options if you don't know where to start but want to enjoy your Mediterranean diet without much hassle. For each of the five weeks included, you will get one breakfast recipe, one lunch recipe, one dinner recipe, and one snack recipe to make meal planning a breeze. So, give these recipes a try! Many of them are so delicious, you'll want to enjoy them over and over again!

Week 1: Success is no accident—you have to reach for it

Mediterranean Breakfast Sandwich

Serves: 4

Time: 20 minutes

Ingredients:

- Baby spinach (2 c.)

- Eggs (4)

- Fresh rosemary (1 Tbsp.)

- Low-fat feta cheese (4 Tbsp.)

- Multigrain sandwich thins (4)

- Olive oil (4 tsp.)

- Salt and pepper according to preference

- Tomato (1, cut into 8 slices)

Instructions:

1. Preheat your oven. This recipe works best at 375° F. Cut the sandwich things in half and brush the insides with half of your olive oil. Place the things on a baking sheet and toast for about five minutes or until the edges are lightly browned and crispy.

2. In a large skillet, heat the rest of your olive oil and the rosemary. Use medium-high heat. Crack your eggs into the skillet one at a time. Cook until the whites have set while keeping the yolks runny. Break the yolks and flip the eggs until done.

3. Serve by placing spinach in between two sandwich thins, along with two tomato slices, an egg, and a tablespoon of feta cheese.

Greek Chicken Bowls

Serves: 4

Time: 20 minutes

Ingredients:

- Arugula (4 c.)
- Chicken breast tenders (1 lb.)

- Cucumber (1, diced)
- Curry powder (1 Tbsp.)
- Dried basil (1 tsp.)
- Garlic powder (1 tsp.)
- Kalamata olives (2 Tbsp.)
- Olive oil (1 Tbsp.)
- Pistachios (0.25 c., chopped)
- Red onion (half, sliced)
- Sunflower seeds (0.25 c.)
- Tzatziki sauce (1 c.)

Instructions:

1. In a bowl, mix in the chicken tenders, curry powder, dried basil, and garlic powder. Make sure to coat the chicken evenly.
2. Heat one tablespoon of olive oil over medium-high. Add the chicken and cook for about four minutes on each side. Remove from the pan and set aside to cool.
3. Place one cup of arugula into four bowls. Toss in the diced cucumber, onion, and kalamata olives.
4. Chop the chicken and distribute evenly between the four bowls.
5. Top with tzatziki sauce, pistachio seeds, and sunflower seeds.

Ratatouille

Serves: 8

Time: 1 hour 30 minutes

Ingredients:

- Crushed tomatoes (1 28 oz. can)
- Eggplants (2)
- Fresh basil (4 Tbsp., chopped)
- Fresh parsley (2 Tbsp., chopped)
- Fresh thyme (2 tsp.)
- Garlic cloves (4, minced and 1 tsp, minced)
- Olive oil (6 Tbsp.)
- Onion (1, diced)
- Red bell pepper (1, diced)
- Roma tomatoes (6)
- Salt and pepper to personal preference
- Yellow bell pepper (1, diced)
- Yellow squashes (2)
- Zucchinis (2)

Instructions:

1. Get your oven ready. This recipe works best at 375° F.
2. Slice the tomatoes, eggplant, squash, and zucchini into thin rounds and set them to the side.

3. Heat up two tablespoons of olive oil in an oven safe pan using medium-high heat. Sauté your onions, four cloves of garlic, and bell peppers for about ten minutes or when soft. Add in your pepper and salt along with the full can of crushed tomatoes. Add in two tablespoons of basil. Stir thoroughly.

4. Take the vegetable slices from earlier and arrange them on top of the sauce in a pattern of your choosing. For example, a slice of eggplant, followed by a slice of tomato, squash, and zucchini, then repeating. Start from the outside and work inward to the center of your pan. Sprinkle salt and pepper overtop the veggies.

5. In a bowl, toss in the remaining basil and garlic, thyme, parsley, salt, pepper, and the rest of the olive oil. Mix it all together, and spoon over the veggies.

6. Cover your pan and bake for 40 minutes. Uncover and then continue baking for another 20 minutes.

Snack Platter

Serves: 6

Time:

Ingredients:

Rosemary Almonds

- Butter (1 Tbsp.)

- Dried rosemary (2 tsp.)
- Salt (pinch)
- Whole almonds (2 c.)

Hummus

- Chickpeas (1 15 oz. can, drained and rinsed)
- Garlic clove (1, peeled)
- Lemon (half, juiced)
- Olive oil (2 Tbsp.)
- Salt and pepper according to personal preference
- Tahini (2 Tbsp.)
- Water (2 Tbsp.)

Other sides

- Bell pepper (1, sliced)
- Cucumber (1, sliced)
- Feta cheese (4 oz, cubed)
- Kalamata olives (handful, drained)
- Pepperoncini peppers (6, drained)
- Pitas (6, sliced into wedges)
- Small fresh mozzarella balls (18)
- Soppressata (6 oz.)
- Sweet cherry peppers (18)

Instructions:

1.   To get started, make your rosemary almonds. Take a large skillet and place it on a burner set to medium heat. Start melting the butter in, then toss in the almonds, rosemary and a bit of salt. Toss the nuts on occasion to ensure even coating.

2.   Cook the almonds for roughly ten minutes, getting them nicely toasted. Set the almonds off to the side to let them cool.

3.   Now you'll set out to make the hummus. Take a blender or food processor and toss in the hummus ingredients. Blend until you get a nice, smooth paste. If you find that your paste is too thick, try blending in a bit of water until you get the desired consistency. Once you have the right consistency, taste for seasoning and adjust as necessary.

4.   Pour and scrape the hummus into a bowl and drizzle in a bit of olive oil. Set it off to the side to get the rest of the platter going.

5.   Grab the sweet cherry peppers and stuff them with the little balls of mozzarella. Arrange a platter in any pattern you like. If serving for a party or family, try keeping each snack in its own little segment to keep things looking neat.

Week 2: Self-belief and effort will take you to what you want to achieve

Breakfast Quesadilla

Serves: 1

Time: 10 minutes

Ingredients:

- Basil (handful)
- Eggs (2)
- Flour tortilla (1)

- Green pesto (1 tsp.)
- Mozzarella (0.25 c.)
- Salt and pepper according to personal preference
- Tomato (half, sliced)

Instructions:

1. Scramble your eggs until just a little runny. Remember, you will be cooking them further inside the quesadilla. Season with salt and pepper.
2. Take the eggs and spread over half of the tortilla.
3. Add basil, pesto, mozzarella cheese, and the slices of tomato.
4. Fold your tortilla and toast on an oiled pan. Toast until both sides are golden brown.

Greek Orzo Salad

Serves: 6

Time: 25 minutes

Ingredients:

- Canned chickpeas (1 c., drained and rinsed)
- Dijon mustard (0.5 tsp)
- Dill (0.33 c., chopped)
- Dried oregano (1 tsp)
- English cucumber (half, diced)
- Feta cheese crumbles (0.5 c.)
- Kalamata olives (0.33 c., halved)
- Lemon (half, juice and zest)
- Mint (0.33 c., chopped)
- Olive oil (3 Tbsp.)
- Orzo pasta (1.25 c. when dry)
- Roasted red pepper (half, diced)
- Salt and pepper to taste
- Shallot (0.25 c., minced)
- White wine vinegar (2 Tbsp.)

Instructions:

1. Prepare the orzo according to the packaging details. Once the orzo is al dente, drain it and rinse until it drops to room temperature.
2. In a bowl, toss all the ingredients together until thoroughly incorporated.

One Pot Mediterranean Chicken

Serves: 4

Time: 1 hour

Ingredients:

- Chicken broth (3 c.)
- Chicken thighs (3, bone in, skin on)

- Chickpeas (1 15 oz can, drained and rinsed)
- Dried oregano (0.5 tsp.)
- Fresh parsley (2 Tbsp., chopped)
- Garlic cloves (2, minced)
- Kalamata olives (0.75 c., halved)
- Olive oil (2 tsp.)
- Onion (1, finely diced)
- Orzo pasta (8 ounces uncooked)
- Roasted peppers (0.5 c., chopped)
- Salt and pepper according to personal preference

Instructions:

1. Prepare your oven at 375°. Heat your olive oil in a large skillet over medium-high heat.
2. Season the chicken with salt and pepper on both sides. Toss the chicken into the skillet and cook for five minutes on each side, or until golden in color. Remove the chicken.
3. Take the skillet and drain most of the rendered fat, leaving about a teaspoon. Add the onion and cook for five minutes. Toss in the garlic and cook for an additional minute.
4. Now you will want to add the orzo, roasted peppers, oregano, chickpeas, and olives into the pan. Add in salt and pepper.
5. Place the thighs on top of the orzo and pour in the chicken broth.
6. Bring to a boil, then cover and place in the oven. Bake for 35 minutes or until chicken has cooked through. Top with parsley and serve.

Mediterranean Nachos

Serves: 6

Time: 10 minutes

Ingredients:

- Canned artichoke hearts (1 c., rinsed, drained, and dried)
- Canned garbanzo beans (0.75 c., rinsed, drained, and dried)
- Feta cheese (0.5 c., crumbled)
- Fresh cilantro (2 Tbsp., chopped)
- Pine nuts (2.5 Tbsp.)
- Roasted red peppers (0.5 c., dried)
- Sabra Hummus (half of their 10 oz. container)
- Tomatoes (0.5 c., chopped)
- Tortilla chips (roughly half a bag)

Instructions:

1. Get your oven ready by setting it to 375°F. In a baking pan, layer the tortilla chips, and spread hummus over them evenly. Top with garbanzo beans, red peppers, artichoke hearts, feta cheese, and pine nuts.
2. Bake for about five minutes or until warmed through. Remove the baking pan and top the nachos with fresh cilantro and tomatoes. Serve and enjoy.

Week 3: The harder you work, the greater the success

Breakfast Tostadas

Serves: 4

Time: 15 minutes

Ingredients:

- Beaten eggs (8)
- Cucumber (0.5 c., seeded and chopped)
- Feta (0.25 c., crumbled)
- Garlic powder (0.5 tsp)
- Green onions (0.5 c., chopped)
- Oregano (0.5 tsp)
- Red Pepper (0.5 c., diced)
- Roasted red pepper hummus (0.5 c.)
- Skim milk (0.5 c.)
- Tomatoes (0.5 c., diced)
- Tostadas (4)

Instructions:

1. In a large skillet, cook the red pepper for two minutes on medium heat until softened. Toss in the eggs, garlic powder, milk, oregano, and green onions. Stir constantly until the egg whites have set.
2. Top the tostadas with hummus, egg mixture, cucumber, feta, and tomatoes.

Roasted Vegetable Bowl

Serves: 2

Time: 45 minutes

Ingredients:

- Crushed red pepper flakes (a pinch)
- Fresh parsley (1 Tbsp., chopped)
- Kalamata olives (0.25 c.)
- Kale (1 c., ribboned)
- Lemon juice (1 Tbsp.)
- Marinated artichoke hearts (0.25 c., drained and chopped)
- Nutritional yeast (1 Tbsp.)
- Olive oil (1 Tbsp., then enough to drizzle)
- Salt and pepper to taste

- Spaghetti squash (half, seeds removed)
- Sun-dried tomatoes (2 Tbsp., chopped)
- Walnuts (0.25 c., chopped)

Instructions:

1. Get your oven ready by setting it to 400° F. Take a baking sheet and blanket it with parchment paper.
2. Take the squash half and place it on the parchment paper. Drizzle olive oil over the side that is cut, and season with salt and pepper. Turn it over so it is facing cut side down and bake for 40 minutes. It is ready when it is soft.
3. Remove the squash shell, and season with a bit more salt and pepper.
4. Stack the kale, artichoke hearts, walnuts, sun-dried tomatoes, and kalamata olives on the squash.
5. Squeeze the lemon juice over and drizzle olive oil. Finish with chopped parsley and a bit of crushed red pepper flakes.

Mediterranean Chicken

Serves: 4

Time: 40 minutes

Ingredients:

- Chicken breasts (1 lb., boneless, skinless)
- Chives (2 Tbsp., chopped)
- Feta cheese (0.25 c., crumbled)
- Garlic (1 tsp., minced)
- Italian seasoning (1 tsp.)
- Lemon juice (2 Tbsp.)
- Olive oil (2 Tbsp., and 1 Tbsp.)
- Salt and pepper according to personal preference
- Tomatoes (1 c., diced)

Instructions:

1. Pour in two tablespoons of olive oil, the lemon juice, salt, pepper, garlic, and Italian seasoning in a resealable plastic bag. Add in the chicken, seal and shake to coat the chicken.
2. Allow the chicken to marinate for at least 30 minutes in the refrigerator.
3. Heat the rest of the olive oil in a pan over medium heat.
4. Place the chicken on the pan and cook for five minutes on each side, or until cooked through.
5. In a bowl, mix the tomatoes, chives, and feta cheese. Season with salt and pepper.
6. When serving, spoon the tomato mixture on top of the chicken.

Baked Phyllo Chips

Serves: 2

Time: 10 minutes

Ingredients:

- Grated cheese (your choice)
- Olive oil (enough to brush with)
- Phyllo sheets (4)
- Salt and pepper according to personal preference

Instructions:

1. Get your oven ready by setting it to 350° F. Brush olive oil over a phyllo sheet generously. Sprinkle grated cheese and your seasoning on top.
2. Grab a second sheet of your phyllo and place it on top of the first one. Again, brush with olive oil and sprinkle cheese and seasoning on top.
3. Repeat this process with the remaining sheets of phyllo. Top the stack with cheese and seasoning.
4. Once complete, cut the stack of phyllo into bite-sized rectangles. A pizza cutter may be helpful here.

5. Grab a baking sheet and blanket it with some parchment paper. Take your phyllo rectangles and place them on the parchment paper.

6. Bake in the oven for about seven minutes or until they reach a golden color.

7. Remove them from the oven and allow them to cool before serving.

Week 4: You don't need perfection—you need effort

Mini Omelets

Serves: 8

Time: 40 minutes

Ingredients:

- Cheddar cheese (0.25 c., shredded)
- Eggs (8)
- Half and half (0.5 c.)
- Olive oil (2 tsps.)
- Salt and pepper according to personal preference
- Spinach (1 c., chopped)

Instructions:

1. Get your oven ready by setting it to 350° F. Prepare a muffin pan or ramekins by greasing them with olive oil.
2. In a bowl, beat the eggs and dairy until you have a fluffy consistency.
3. Stir in the cheese and your seasonings. Pour in the spinach and continue beating the eggs.
4. Pour the egg mixture into your ramekins or muffin pan.
5. Bake the omelets until they have set, which should be roughly 25 minutes. Remove them from the oven and allow them to cool before serving.

Basil Shrimp Salad

Serves: 2

Time: 40 minutes

Ingredients:

- Dried basil (1 tsp.)
- Lemon juice (1 Tbsp.)
- Olive oil (1 tsp.)
- Romaine lettuce (2 c.)
- Shrimp (12 medium or 8 large)
- White wine vinegar (0.25 c.)

Instructions:

1. Whisk together the white wine vinegar, olive oil, lemon juice, and basil. Stick your shrimp in the marinade for half an hour.

2. Take the marinade and shrimp and cook in a skillet over medium heat until cooked through.

3. Allow the shrimp to cool along with the juice and pour into a bowl. Toss in the romaine lettuce and mix well to get the flavor thoroughly infused in the salad. Serve.

Mediterranean Flounder

Serves: 4

Time: 40 minutes

Ingredients:

- Capers (0.25 c.)
- Diced tomatoes (1 can)
- Flounder fillets (1 lb.)
- Fresh basil (12 leaves, chopped)
- Fresh parmesan cheese (3 Tbsp., grated)
- Garlic cloves (2, chopped)
- Italian seasoning (a pinch)
- Kalamata olives (0.5 c., pitted and chopped)
- Lemon juice (1 tsp.)

- Red onion (half, chopped)
- White wine (0.25 c.)

Instructions:

1. Set your oven to 425° F. Take a skillet and pour in enough olive oil to sauté the onion until soft. Cook on medium-high heat.
2. Toss in the garlic, Italian seasoning, and tomatoes. Cook for an additional five minutes.
3. Pour in the wine, capers, olives, lemon juice, and only half of the basil you chopped.
4. Reduce the heat to low and stir in the parmesan cheese. Simmer for ten minutes or until the sauce has thickened.
5. Place the flounder fillets in a baking pan and pour the sauce over top. Sprinkle the remaining basil on top and bake for 12 minutes.

Nutty Energy Bites

Serves: 10

Time: 10 minutes

Ingredients:

- Dried dates (1 c., pitted)
- Almonds (0.5 c.)

- Pine nuts (0.25 c.)

- Flaxseeds (1 Tbsp., milled) Porridge oats (2 Tbsp.)

- Pistachios (0.25 c., coarsely ground)

Instructions:

1. Take the dates, pine nuts, milled flaxseeds, almonds, and porridge oats and pour them into a food processor or blender. Mix until thoroughly incorporated.

2. Using a tablespoon, scoop the mixture and roll it between your hands until you have a small, bite-sized ball. Do this until you have used the entirety of the dough. This recipe should be enough for about ten.

3. On a plate, sprinkle your ground pistachios. Take the energy balls and roll them on the pistachio grounds, making sure to coat them evenly. Serve or store in the refrigerator.

Week 5: Transformation Happens One Day at a Time

Mediterranean Breakfast Bowl

Serves: 1

Time: 25 minutes

Ingredients:

- Artichoke hearts (0.25 c., chopped)
- Baby arugula (2 c.)
- Capers (1 Tbsp.)
- Egg (1)
- Feta (2 Tbsp., crumbled)
- Garlic (0.25 tsp)
- Kalamata olives (5, chopped)
- Lemon thyme (1 Tbsp., chopped)
- Olive oil (0.5 Tbsp.)
- Pepper (0.25 tsp)
- Sun-dried tomatoes (2 Tbsp., chopped)
- Sweet potato (1 c., cubed)

Instructions:

1. Take your olive oil and, when hot, pan fry your sweet potatoes for 5-10 minutes until they have softened. Then, sprinkle on the seasonings.
2. Place arugula into a bowl, then top with potatoes, then everything but the egg.
3. Prepare the egg to your liking and serve.

Chicken Shawarma Pita Pockets

Serves: 6

Time: 40 minutes

Ingredients:

- Cayenne (0.5 tsp)
- Chicken thighs (8, boneless, skinless, bite-sized pieces)
- Cloves (0.5 tsp, ground)
- Garlic powder (0.75 Tbsp.)
- Ground cumin (0.75 Tbsp.)
- Lemon juice (1 lemon)
- Olive oil (0.33 c.)
- Onion (1, sliced thinly)
- Paprika (0.75 Tbsp.)
- Salt
- Turmeric powder (0.75 Tbsp.)

To serve:

- Pita pockets (6)
- Tzatziki sauce
- Arugula
- Diced tomatoes
- Diced onions

- Sliced Kalamata olives

Instructions:

1. Combine all spices. Then, place all chicken, already diced, into the bowl. Coat well, then toss in onions, lemon juice, and oil. Mix well and let marinade for at least 3 hours, or overnight.
2. Preheat the oven to 425 F. Allow chicken to sit at room temperature a few minutes. Then, spread it on an oiled sheet pan. Roast for 30 minutes.
3. To serve, fill up a pita pocket with tzatziki, chicken, arugula, and any toppings you prefer. Enjoy.

Turkey Mediterranean Casserole

Serves: 6

Time: 35 minutes

Ingredients:

- Fusilli pasta (0.5 lbs.)
- Turkey (1.5 c., chopped)
- Sun dried tomatoes (2 Tbsp., drained)
- Canned artichokes (7 oz., drained)
- Kalamata olives (3.5 oz., drained and chopped)
- Parsley (0.5 Tbsp., chopped and fresh)
- Basil (1 T, fresh)

- Salt and pepper to taste
- Marinara sauce (1 c.)
- Black chopped olives (2 oz., drained)
- Mozzarella cheese (1.5 c., shredded)

Instructions:

1. Warm your oven to 350 F. Prepare your pasta according to the directions, drain, and place into a bowl. Prepare your basil, parsley, olives, tomatoes, artichokes, and other ingredients.

2. Mix together the pasta with the turkey, tomatoes, olives, artichokes, herbs, seasoning, and marinara sauce. Give it a good mix to incorporate all of the ingredients evenly.

3. Take a 9x13 oven-safe dish and layer in the first half of your pasta mixture. Then, sprinkle on half of your mozzarella cheese. Top with the rest of the pasta, then sprinkle on the chopped black olives as well. Spread the rest of the shredded cheese on top, then bake it for 20-25 minutes. It is done when the cheese is all bubbly and the casserole is hot.

Heirloom Tomato and Cucumber Toast

Serves: 2

Time: 5 minutes

Ingredients:

- Heirloom tomato (1, diced)
- Persian cucumber (1, diced)
- Extra virgin olive oil (1 tsp)
- Oregano (a pinch, dried)
- Kosher salt and pepper
- Whipped cream cheese (2 tsp)
- Whole grain bread (2 pieces)
- Balsamic glaze (1 tsp)

Instructions:

4. Combine the tomato, cucumber, oil, and all seasonings together.
5. Spread cheese across bread, then top with mixture, followed by balsamic glaze.

Chapter 3: Maintaining Your Diet

Sticking to a diet can be tough. You could see that other people are having some great food and wish that you could enjoy it too. You might realize that you miss the foods that you used to eat and feel like it's a drag to not be able to enjoy them. When you are able to enjoy the foods that you are eating, sticking to your diet is far easier. However, that doesn't mean that you won't miss those old foods sometimes. Thankfully, the Mediterranean diet is not a very restrictive one—you are able to enjoy foods in moderation that would otherwise not be allowed, and because of that, you can take the slice of cake at the work party, or you can choose to pick up a coffee for yourself every now and then. When you do this, you're not doing anything wrong, so long as you enjoy food in moderation.

Within this chapter, we are going to take a look at several tips that you can use that will help you with maintaining your diet so that you will be able to stick to it, even when you feel like things are getting difficult. Think of this as your guide to avoiding giving in entirely—this will help you to do the best thing for yourself so that you can know that you are healthy. Now, let's get started.

Find Your Motivation

First, if you want to keep yourself on your diet, one of the best things that you can do is make sure that you find and stick to your motivation. Make sure that you know what it is in life that is motivating you. Are you losing weight because a doctor told you to? Fair enough—but how do you make that personal and about yourself? Maybe instead of looking at it as a purely health-related choice, look at it as something that you are doing because of yourself. Maybe you are eating better so that you are able to watch your children graduate or so that you can run after them at the park and stay healthy, even when it is hard to do so.

Remind Yourself Why You are Eating Healthily

When you find that you are struggling to eat healthily, remind yourself of why you are doing it in the first place. When you do this enough, you will begin to resist the urges easier than ever. Make it a point to tell yourself not to eat something a certain way. Take the time to remind yourself that you don't need to order that greasy pizza—you are eating better foods because you want to be there for your children or grandchildren.

Reminding yourself of your motivation is a great way to overcome those cravings that you may have at any point in time. The cravings that you have are usually strong and compelling, but if you learn to overcome them, you realize that they weren't actually as powerful as you thought they were. Defeat the cravings. Learn to tell yourself that they are not actually able to control you. Tell yourself that you can do better with yourself.

Eat Slowly

Now, on the Mediterranean diet, you should already be eating your meals with other people anyway. You should be taking the time to enjoy those meals while talking to other people and ensuring that you get that connection with them, and in doing so, you realize that you are able to do better. You realize that you are able to keep yourself under control longer, and that is a great way to defend and protect yourself from overeating.

When you eat slowly, you can get the same effect. Eating slowly means that you will have longer for your brain to realize that you should be eating less. When you are able to trigger that sensation of satiety because you were eating slowly, you end up eating fewer calories by default, and that matters immensely.

Keep Yourself Accountable

Don't forget that, ultimately, your diet is something that you must control on your own. Keep yourself accountable by making sure that you show other people what you are doing. If you are trying to lose weight, let them know, and tell them how you plan to do so. When you do this, you are able to remind yourself that other people know what you are doing and why—this is a great way to foster that sense of accountability because you will feel like you have to actually follow through, or you will be embarrassed by having to admit fault. You could also make accountability to yourself as well. When you do this, you are able to remind yourself that your diet is your own. Using apps to track your food and caloric intake is just one way that you can do this.

Remember Your Moderation

While it can be difficult to face a diet where you feel like you can't actually enjoy the foods that you would like to eat, the truth is that on the Mediterranean diet, you are totally okay to eat those foods that you like or miss if you do so in moderation. There is nothing that is absolutely forbidden on the Mediterranean diet—there are just foods that you should be restricting regularly. However, that doesn't mean that you can't have a treat every now and then.

Remembering to live in moderation will help you from feeling like you have to cheat or give up as well. When you are able to enjoy your diet and still enjoy the times where you want to enjoy your treats, you realize that there is actually a happy medium between sticking to the diet and deciding to quit entirely.

Identify the Difference between Hunger and Craving

Another great way to help yourself stick to your diet is to recognize that there is a very real difference between actually being hungry and just craving something to eat. In general, cravings are felt in the mouth—when you feel like you are salivating or like you need to eat something, but it is entirely in your head and mouth, you know that you have a craving. When you are truly hungry, you feel an emptiness in your stomach—you are able to know because your abdomen is where the motivation is coming from.

Being able to tell when you have a craving and when you are genuinely hungry,

235

you can usually avoid eating extra calories that you didn't actually need. This is major—if you don't want to overeat, you need to know when your body actually needs something and when it just wants something. And if you find that you just want something, that's okay too—just find a way to move on from it. If you want to indulge a bit here and there, there's no harm in that!

Stick to the Meal Plan

When it comes to sticking to a diet, one of the easiest and most straightforward ways to do so is to just stick to your meal plan that you set up. You have it there for a reason—it is there for you to fall back on, and the sooner that you are willing to accept that, recognizing that ultimately, you can stay on track when you don't have to think about things too much, the better you will do. You will be able to succeed on your diet because you will know that you have those tools in place to protect you—they will be lined up to ensure that your diet is able to provide you with everything that you need and they will also be there so that you can know that you are on the right track.

Drink Plenty of Water

Another key to keeping yourself on track with your diet is to make sure that you drink plenty of water throughout the day. Oftentimes, we mistake our thirst with hunger and eat instead. Of course, if you're thirsty, food isn't going to really fix your problem, and you will end up continuing to mix up the sensation as you try to move past it. The more you eat, the thirstier you will get until you realize that you're full but still feeling "hungry." By drinking plenty of water any time that you think that you might want to eat, you will be able to keep yourself hydrated, and in addition, you will prevent yourself from unintentionally eating too much.

Eat Several Times Per Day

One of the best ways to keep yourself on track with your diet is to make sure that you are regularly eating. By eating throughout the day, making sure that you keep yourself full, it is easier to keep yourself strong enough to resist giving in to cravings or anything else. When you do this regularly, you will discover that you can actually keep away much of your cravings so that you are more successful in managing your diet.

Eating several times per day often involves small meals and snacks if you prefer to do so. Some people don't like doing this, but if you find that you're one of those people who will do well on a diet when you are never actually hungry enough to get desperate enough to break it, you will probably be just fine.

Fill Up on Protein

Another great way to protect yourself from giving in and caving on your diet is to make sure that you fill up on protein. Whether it comes from an animal or plant source, make sure that every time you eat, you have some sort of tangible protein source. This is the best way to keep yourself on track because protein keeps you fuller for longer. When you eat something that's loaded up with protein, you don't feel the need to eat as much later on. The protein is usually very dense, and that means that you get to resist feeling hungry for longer than you thought that you would.

Some easy proteins come from nuts—but make sure that you are mindful that you do not end up overeating during this process—you might unintentionally end up eating too many without realizing it. While you should be eating proteins regularly, make sure that you are mindful of calorie content as well!

Keep Only Healthy Foods

A common mistake that people make while dieting is that they end up caving when they realize that their home is filled up with foods that they shouldn't be eating. Perhaps you are the only person in your home that is attempting to diet. In this case, you may end up running into a situation where you have all sorts of non-compliant foods on hand. You might have chips for your kids or snacks that your partner likes to eat on hand. You may feel like it is difficult for you to stay firm when you have that to consider, and that means that you end up stuck in temptation.

One of the best ways to prevent this is to either cut all of the unhealthy junk out of your home entirely or make sure that you keep the off-limits foods in specific places so that you don't have to look at it and see it tempting you every time that you go to get a snack for yourself. By trying to keep yourself limited to just healthy foods, you will be healthier, and you will make better decisions.

Eat Breakfast Daily

Finally, make sure that breakfast is non-negotiable. Make sure that you enjoy it every single day, even if you're busy. This is where those make-ahead meals can come in handy; by knowing that you have to keep to a meal plan and knowing that you already have the food on hand, you can keep yourself fed. Breakfast sets you up for success or failure—if you want to truly succeed on your diet, you must make sure that you are willing to eat those healthier foods as much as possible, and you must get started on the right foot. Enjoy those foods first thing every day. Eat so that you are not ravenous when you finally do decide that it is time to sit down and find something to eat. Even if you just have a smoothie or something quick to eat as you go, having breakfast will help you to persevere.

CPSIA information can be obtained
at www.ICGtesting.com
Printed in the USA
BVHW091523170921
616966BV00006B/396

9 789814 950725